Applied Akka Patterns
A Hands-On Guide to Designing
Distributed Applications

Michael Nash and Wade Waldron

Beijing · Boston · Farnham · Sebastopol · Tokyo

Applied Akka Patterns

by Michael Nash and Wade Waldron

Printed in the United States of America.

Published by O'Reilly Media, Inc., 1005 Gravenstein Highway North, Sebastopol, CA 95472.

O'Reilly books may be purchased for educational, business, or sales promotional use. Online editions are also available for most titles (*http://oreilly.com/safari*). For more information, contact our corporate/institutional sales department: 800-998-9938 or *corporate@oreilly.com*.

Editors: Nan Barber and Brian Foster
Production Editor: Kristen Brown
Copyeditor: Octal Publishing, Inc.
Proofreader: Jasmine Kwityn

Indexer: Angela Howard
Interior Designer: David Futato
Cover Designer: Karen Montgomery
Illustrator: Rebecca Demarest

December 2016:   First Edition

Revision History for the First Edition
2016-12-09:   First Release

See *http://oreilly.com/catalog/errata.csp?isbn=9781491934883* for release details.

978-1-491-93488-3

[LSI]

Table of Contents

Preface

Reactive Application Development is the new frontier of software development. As the prevalence of connected devices has increased, so has the amount of data available. Older techniques for processing that data in a single-threaded batch simply can't hold up under the demands presented by this new world. Big data is on the rise and we need new tools and new techniques to deal with it.

Often, the solution to modern problems doesn't come from the present, but rather from the past. Many of today's new tools for processing big data are in fact based on the older concept of actors. Actors are the key concept from which Akka was built, but it has its roots in the past. It isn't a new concept; rather, it's an old one brought to light in the modern world.

As we set forth to explore Akka, actors, streams, and all the other things associated with them, we will be approaching them from the perspective of a real-world concern: the problem of how to schedule a group of people across a variety of projects while optimizing both for the time they have available, as well as their skill sets. This is a complex problem, not one easily solved in an afternoon. But it is an interesting issue that provides a lot of room for depth. It is also a problem that most software developers will be involved with at some point during their career. We will refer back to this problem throughout our exploration of Akka.

But before we get to solving the problems of our domain, we have to first understand the tools that we have available. We also need to understand why those tools exist, and what kinds of problems they were intended to solve. We need to know the origin of Akka, with its roots in the Actor Model. We need a guiding set of principles to help us stitch together our application, found in our exploration of domain-driven design (DDD). From there, we can begin to build out our domain, using all of the tools Akka provides. We can explore the use of simple actors and how they relate to streams. We can take our system and distribute across multiple nodes, providing better fault tolerance, availability, and of course, scalability.

But first, we need to know where it all came from.

Conventions Used in This Book

The following typographical conventions are used in this book:

Italic
>   Indicates new terms, URLs, email addresses, filenames, and file extensions.

`Constant width`
>   Used for program listings, as well as within paragraphs to refer to program elements such as variable or function names, databases, data types, environment variables, statements, and keywords.

`Constant width bold`
>   Shows commands or other text that should be typed literally by the user.

`Constant width italic`
>   Shows text that should be replaced with user-supplied values or by values determined by context.

 This element signifies a tip or suggestion.

 This element signifies a general note.

 This element indicates a warning or caution.

O'Reilly Safari

 *Safari* (formerly Safari Books Online) is membership-based training and reference platform for enterprise, government, educators, and individuals.

Members have access to thousands of books, training videos, Learning Paths, interactive tutorials, and curated playlists from over 250 publishers, including O'Reilly

Media, Harvard Business Review, Prentice Hall Professional, Addison-Wesley Professional, Microsoft Press, Sams, Que, Peachpit Press, Adobe, Focal Press, Cisco Press, John Wiley & Sons, Syngress, Morgan Kaufmann, IBM Redbooks, Packt, Adobe Press, FT Press, Apress, Manning, New Riders, McGraw-Hill, Jones & Bartlett, and Course Technology, among others.

For more information, please visit *http://oreilly.com/safari*.

How to Contact Us

Please address comments and questions concerning this book to the publisher:

>O'Reilly Media, Inc.
>1005 Gravenstein Highway North
>Sebastopol, CA 95472
>800-998-9938 (in the United States or Canada)
>707-829-0515 (international or local)
>707-829-0104 (fax)

We have a web page for this book, where we list errata, examples, and any additional information. You can access this page at *http://bit.ly/applied_akka_patterns*.

To comment or ask technical questions about this book, send email to *bookquestions@oreilly.com*.

For more information about our books, courses, conferences, and news, see our website at *http://www.oreilly.com*.

Find us on Facebook: *http://facebook.com/oreilly*

Follow us on Twitter: *http://twitter.com/oreillymedia*

Watch us on YouTube: *http://www.youtube.com/oreillymedia*

Acknowledgments

We would like to thank the many people who helped make this book possible, including the Akka team, both within Lightbend and in the greater community, as well as our editor, Nan Barber, and our reviewers, Konrad Malawski, Sean Glover, and Petro Verkhogliad. We especially want to thank our families for their patience and support.

CHAPTER 1

The Actor Model

It is essential to understand how actors were *meant* to be used to realize their full value, and that's what you will learn in this chapter. Here, we explore actors—how they work, and how they interact with one another and the outside world.

Many of the techniques we use to design software teach you that it is important to look at the real world before writing code. We must understand the use case for the software. We need to ask questions about who will be using it and how they will use it. These questions are critical to the design of good software. But in the pursuit of our design, we often forget to ask ourselves an important question: "How long will it take?" Yet, anyone who has written a highly concurrent system knows that time is an integral part of how we develop our software.

Let's explore a bit far afield from software for a moment—don't worry, we'll show how this relates to software development in a moment!

Reality Is Eventually Consistent

Consider the example of reaching for a cup of coffee. On the surface, this might seem like a very simple example. You reach out and pick up a cup of coffee. Not much is happening there. But let's look deeper.

To be able to pick up the coffee, you need to know where it is. You can look over and see the cup, but are you seeing it as it is, or as it was? The information you use to determine the location of the cup is based on the photons reflected from that cup. Those photons take time to travel. Further, when our eyes receive the data, they must perform some processing before sending the data to our brain. Further processing needs to be done by other areas of our nervous system in order to communicate the desire to move our arm. Finally, our arm must stretch out to take the cup.

At each stage in the process, small amounts of delay have leaked into the system. Picking up a coffee cup is a fairly simple operation, though, in a very static environment, so those delays don't have a large effect. But as the nature of the environment changes, as events begin to happen faster and more frequently, those small delays can add up. Picking up a cup of coffee is fairly trivial. Trying to catch that same cup of coffee if it falls off the table, without spilling it, is much more challenging. Trying to catch multiple cups…well, now we've entered the realm of the impossible.

The truth is that our reality is bounded by the speed of light. The laws of physics, and the speed of light, put an upper bound on causality. Unless two things occupy the same space (which, of course, is impossible), for one event to have an effect on another, there must be a passage of time between the two. Two observers watching the same event from different distances will experience that event at different times. The person closer to the event will experience it first, while the person further away will experience it slightly later. Yet, despite the difference in time, both experiences are real. Both are equally valid. It is this idea, rooted in physics, on which the Actor Model is based.

The truth is that we live our lives operating on out-of-date information. On a small scale, our cells are communicating with one another through messages passed in the form of hormones. On a larger scale, we go through our daily lives talking to people, watching the news, reading the latest developments on a blog. All of these things are in one way or another just a form of asynchronous messaging. In fact, when we break it down, there is nothing in our lives that is being experienced synchronously.

Even our computers behave this way. Every operation a computer performs is done by sending a signal over some kind of medium, whether it's electrical signals, photons, or something else.

So, if everything in the world is being experienced in an asynchronous manner, why do we put so much effort into trying to write software that is synchronous? We teach ourselves that we should model software on the real world, yet we ignore the fundamental concept of time. Wouldn't it be better if we modeled it on the real world and built our software using asynchronous events or messages?

As a fun exercise, let's reverse this idea. Let's take the real world and model it through the lens of traditional synchronous software. How does this look? What are the consequences?

Let's go back to our coffee example. When your brain decides that you want a sip of coffee, it must first pause time, at least in a localized fashion. You need to halt the world around you so that you can ensure that nothing changes between the moment you decide to have that coffee and the moment when the coffee reaches your lips. Nothing can interfere with that. If you reach out to take the coffee, only to discover someone else got there first, you have chaos. Instead, you freeze everything around you, locking the state in place, so that you can guarantee that won't happen. Anyone else who might have been reaching for that same cup will now be stopped, frozen until you have completed your action. This means not just pausing another person, but also pausing the air, the light, everything around that cup. Everything between the cup and you must stop, or else your state might become invalid. This sounds very complicated, much more complicated than if we had just taken the time to model the system correctly in the first place.

This is one of the fundamentals of the Actor Model—with it, we can build software that reflects how reality actually works instead of assuming a frozen-in-time world that doesn't actually exist.

Deconstructing the Actor Model

In 1973, Carl Hewitt, along with Peter Bishop and Richard Steiger, set out to help solve some of these problems in a paper called "Universal Modular Actor Formalism for Artificial Intelligence." Although many programming paradigms are based around mathematical models, the Actor Model was, according to Hewitt, inspired by physics. It has evolved over the years, but the fundamental concepts have stayed the same.

It is important to understand that when working with Akka, you can write code without using the Actor Model. The fact that you are using actors does not imply that you are using the Actor Model. There are many developers who have been using Akka for years and are unaware of the Actor Model.

The difference between using the Actor Model and simply using actors is the way that you treat those actors. If you use those actors as the top-level building blocks, such that all code in your system resides within a system of actors, you are using the Actor Model. On the other hand, if you build your system such that you have actors residing within nonactors, then you are not using the Actor Model.

It is also important to understand that programming in the Actor Model is not about any one tool or technology. Entire languages have been written around the idea of the Actor Model. In this way, it is more like a programming paradigm than a set of tools. Learning it is like learning object-oriented programming (OOP) or functional programming. And like those two methodologies, the Actor Model predates Akka, and there are many other implementations of it.

The Pony language, for instance, is based on actors and can be easily used to implement the Actor Model. Erlang's processes are equivalent to Akka actors; they are a fundamental feature of Erlang. In Ada, the idea of the Task exists, along with messages called "entries"—which are queued by the asynchronous Tasks—meaning the Actor Model can be implemented in this language, as well.

To implement the Actor Model, there are a few fundamental rules to follow:

- All computation is performed within an actor
- Actors can communicate only through messages
- In response to a message, an actor can:
  - Change its state or behavior
  - Send messages to other actors
  - Create a finite number of child actors

Of course, if you are familiar with Akka, you can immediately recognize how these components have been implemented, but let's talk about them outside of that context for a moment so that we can better understand how the basic Actor Model might differ from the Akka implementation.

All Computation Is Performed Within an Actor

Carl Hewitt called the actor the fundamental unit of computation.[1] What does it mean to be the fundamental unit of computation? It means that when you build a system using the Actor Model, everything is an actor. Whether you are computing a Fibonacci sequence or maintaining the state of a user in your system, you do so within an actor, or multiple actors.

This idea that everything is an actor is not without difficulties, though. If every computation needs to happen within an actor, this implies that every function and every state variable could be its own actor. And even though this is technically possible, it's not always pragmatic. Often, we have groups of related functions and it is usually more convenient to wrap all those functions within a single actor. Doing so doesn't violate the Actor Model. But how do we decide where to draw the line? We will discuss this in more detail in Chapter 3 when we learn about domain-driven design (DDD). The building blocks we introduce for DDD are excellent candidates to turn into actors and we can use them as guiding principles for when to create a new actor.

Actors in the Actor Model embody not only state but also behavior. This might sound suspiciously like the definition of OOP—in fact the two are very closely related. Alan Kay, who coined the term "object-oriented programming" and was one of the original creators of the Smalltalk language, was largely influenced by the Actor Model. And while Smalltalk and OOP eventually evolved away from their Actor Model roots, many of the basic principles of the Actor Model remain in our modern interpretation of OOP. In truth, the original focus of OOP was not the objects themselves but rather the messages flowing between them.

---

1 For more on this, see the video "Hewitt, Meijer and Szyperski: The Actor Model (everything you wanted to know…)" (*https://www.youtube.com/watch?v=7erJ1DV_Tlo*).

OOP models the fundamental unit of computation as an object (an instance of a class), and is familiar to developers coming from Java and similar languages. Functional programming, on the other hand, models computation around functions and their applications, and is seen in languages such as Lisp and Haskell.

Another aspect of the model that is useful for highly concurrent applications is the idea that an actor's state is isolated. It is never directly exposed to the outside world. We don't allow actors to look at or modify the state of another actor, except indirectly through messages. This isolation applies equally to the actor's behavior. The internal methods or mechanisms of the actor are never exposed to other actors. In fact, state and behavior can largely be treated as the same thing within an actor (more on this later).

Actors in the model can take many different forms. They can exist as highly technical constructs like a database access layer, or they can be domain-specific constructs like a person or schedule. They can even be used to perform simple mathematical operations. Anything in the system that needs to perform any amount of computation is an actor.

The actor is the fundamental building block in the Actor Model as well as Akka-based applications, as we will see.

Actors Can Communicate Only Through Messages

We have created our actors in an isolated fashion so that they never expose their state or their behavior. This is an important element of the Actor Model. Because we have isolated them in this way, we need to find other ways by which we can communicate with them and learn about the state of the system.

Messages are the backbone of all communication in the Actor Model. They are what enables communication *between* actors.

Every actor, when created, is given an address. This address is the entry point for communication with that actor. You cannot use the address to access the actor directly, but you can use it to send messages to that actor.

Akka separates the concept of an address from a reference. Most actor communication is done using references. Akka actors also have an address that can be used in some circumstances; however, they are generally avoided. Nonetheless, whether you are using a reference or an address, the basic principle is the same: you have a means to locate the mailbox for the actor so that you can deliver a message to it.

Messages that are sent to an actor are pieces of immutable data. These messages are sent to a mailbox that exists at the address provided for the destination actor. What happens after the message reaches the mailbox is beyond the control of the sender. Messages can be delivered out of order, or they might not even be delivered at all. The Actor Model provides an *At Most Once* guarantee of delivery. This means that failure is an option, and if we need to guarantee delivery, we will need other tools to enable that.

At Most Once delivery is the default guarantee provided by the Actor Model and by Akka. However, At Least Once delivery can be built on top of At Most Once delivery, and there are mechanisms within Akka to provide that.

Akka further provides a slightly stronger guarantee of ordering. In Akka, message order is guaranteed between any pair of actors. That is, if one actor sends multiple messages to another, we can guarantee that the order of those messages will be preserved.

After the messages are in the mailbox, the actor can receive those messages. However, messages are received one at a time. No single actor can process two messages simultaneously. This is a critical guarantee because it allows us to operate within the actor in a *single-threaded illusion*. Actors are free to modify their internal state with no worries about whether another thread might also be operating on that state. As long as we maintain the single-threaded illusion, our state is protected against any of the normal concerns of concurrency.

The exact nature of the messages is dependent on the actor's functionality. For domain actors, it would be common to see the messages as commands or events presented by using domain terms like "AddUser" or "CreateProject" in our scheduling example. Of course, if the actor is more technical in nature, the messages can be more technical, like "Save" or "Compute."

Because actors communicate only through messages, it allows for some interesting options. As long as the actor on the other end of the mailbox is able to process the message, it can take any form necessary to get the job done (Figure 1-1). This means that the receiving actor can process the message directly or it can act as a proxy for the message, simply forwarding it on to another actor to do the necessary work. It might also break the message into smaller chunks, sending those chunks on to other actors (or possibly itself) to be processed. In this way, the details of how the message is processed can be as simple or as complex as required, and the details of this implementation are transparent to the sender of the message.

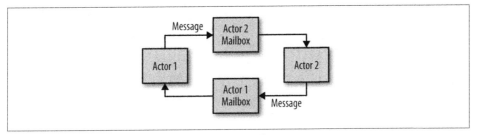

Figure 1-1. Actors communicating with one another

 It is worth mentioning that Akka treats its mailboxes slightly differently. The default implementation in Akka provides an ordered mailbox so that you can guarantee that messages will be processed by the actor in the order in which they are placed in the mailbox.

Actors Can Create Child Actors

In the Actor Model, everything is an actor, and actors can communicate only through messages. But actors also need to know that other actors exist.

One of the actions that is available to an actor when it receives a message is that it can create a finite number of child actors. The parent will then know about the child actor(s) and will have access to the child's address. This means that a parent actor can send messages to a child actor.

In addition to knowing about actors by creating them as children, an actor can pass the address to another actor through a message. In this way, a parent could inform a child about any other actor the parent is aware of, including itself. Thus, a child actor can know the address of its parent or siblings with very little difficulty. With a little more work, the child can know about other actors that exist in the hierarchy, as well. In addition, if the address used for the actor follows a set pattern, it is possible to synthesize addresses for other actors, though this can create undesirable complexity, and possibly security concerns, if not used carefully.

This hierarchy of actors means that with the exception of the root, all actors will have a parent and any actor can have one or more children. The collection of these actors, starting from the root and working down through the tree, is called an *actor system.*

Each actor in the actor system can always be uniquely identified by its address. It is not critical that it follow any particular pattern, so long as the address can be guaranteed to uniquely identify an actor. Akka uses a hierarchical pattern of naming, much like a directory structure (similar to that shown in Figure 1-2), or you could use randomly generated unique keys.

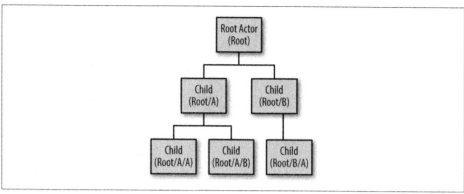

Figure 1-2. A hierarchical system of actors

In Figure 1-2, the *root* actor is the top-level actor under which all others will be created. The root actor then has two children A and B. The address for A is Root/A and the address for B is Root/B. Beneath A are two more actors named A and B. Even though these share the name of other actors, their address is still unique (Root/A/A and Root/A/B). Child B also has a child of its own with the path Root/B/A. Again, the address is unique, even if the name is not. This is just one example of how addresses can be created.

Child actors are one of the most valuable integration techniques in the Actor Model, and also form the basis of actor supervision in Akka, as we will see.

Actors Can Change Their State or Behavior

In addition to sending messages and creating child actors, actors can also change how they will react to the next message. We often use the term "behavior" when talking about how an actor will change, but this is slightly misleading. The change in behavior, or the change in how an actor will react, can also manifest itself as a change of state.

Let's consider the scheduling example discussed in the introduction. If we have an actor that represents a person's availability, the initial state might indicate that this person is available for a project. When a message comes in to assign that person to a project, the actor can alter itself such that when a new message comes in, it will show as unavailable. Even though this seems to be a change in state, we still consider it to be a change to the actor's behavior because the actor is now behaving like it has a value of unavailable when the next message comes in.

We can also have an actor that changes the computation that it will perform when it receives the next message. The actor representing a person in this system might be able to exist in different states. While that person is employed and available to be on a project, they can exist in an Active state. However, certain conditions can result in that person moving to an Inactive state (termination, extended leave, etc.). While in an Active state, project requests can be processed as normal. However, if a message comes into the actor that puts it into an Inactive state, the system might begin rejecting project requests. In this case, the actor alters the computation that it performs when the next message comes in.

Because actors can alter their behavior and state using this method, it makes them an excellent tool for modeling finite-state machines. Each behavior in the system can represent a state, and the actor can move from one state to the next when it receives a message.

Figure 1-3 shows a simple finite-state machine representing a person in the system. In this example, a person can exist in a limited set of states. He can be Created (but not yet Active), Active, Inactive, or Terminated. When a person is created in the system, he enters the Created state. In this state, he is not yet Active. This might occur when the person has been hired but has not yet begun employment, for example. After a person becomes Active, he can't go back to the Created state. An Active person can be scheduled to work on a project. At some point, that person might become Inactive, perhaps because he goes on leave. While Inactive, the person cannot accept any requests. He can move freely between the Active and Inactive states. Eventually, the person might leave the company, at which point the system moves the person to the Terminated state. After a person enters the Terminated state, he cannot go back to the Active or Inactive states. He can go from the Terminated state to Created to accommodate the possibility that the person is rehired later on.

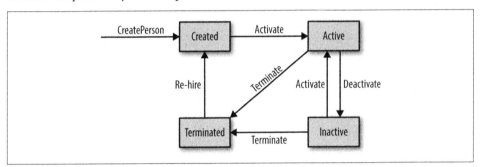

Figure 1-3. A finite-state machine using actors

 Actors are an excellent way to model a finite-state machine and are commonly used in this way. Akka provides specific tools that make the creation of finite-state machines easier in the form of the Akka FSM.

We obviously can create far more complex scenarios, but this gives you an idea of the types of things that you can accomplish by altering the behavior of an actor. Whether it is altering the messages that are accepted, altering the way those messages are handled, or altering the state of the actor, this all falls under the heading of behavior. Akka provides several sophisticated techniques for altering actor behavior, as we will discuss in detail.

Everything Is an Actor

Now that you understand the building blocks of an actor and of a system of actors, let's return to the idea that everything is an actor and see what that means, and what it looks like.

Let's consider our scheduling domain again. A person in our scheduling domain will have a variety of associated information. Each person might have a schedule indicating availability. Of course, that schedule would break down further into more discrete time periods.

In a more traditional object-oriented architecture, you might have a class to represent the person. That class would then have a schedule class associated with it. And that schedule might break down further into individual dates. When a request comes into the system, it would call functions on the person class, which would in turn call functions on the schedule class and the individual dates.

The Actor Model version of this isn't much different, except now you have an actor representing the person. But in the Actor Model, the schedule can also be an actor because it potentially makes a computation. Each individual date can also be an actor because they might also need to make a computation. In fact, it is possible that the request itself can have an actor associated with it. In some cases, the request might need to aggregate information as it is computed by the other pieces of the model. In this case, we might want to create a `RequestWorker` that will handle the aggregation.

As Figure 1-4 shows, in this model, instead of calling functions that will alter the state of the objects, you pass messages between them. Messages like `CheckAvailability` flow from the `Person` actor into the `ScheduleActor` actor. In this example, the `Person` represents the topmost actor. The `Schedule` is a child of `Person`, and the individual `Dates` are children of the `Schedule`. And because we are using the Actor Model, all messages are handled concurrently. This way, we can compute multiple dates in the schedule at the same time; we don't need to wait for one to complete before moving on to the next. In fact, we don't even need to complete the previous request before starting on the next one. The schedule can be working on two simultaneous requests, each looking at overlapping dates. Due to the single-threaded illusion, if two requests try to schedule the same date, only the first request will succeed. This happens because the same actor is used to process both requests for that date, and the actor can process only one message at a time. On the other hand, if there is no overlap in dates, both requests can be processed and completed simultaneously, allowing us to make better use of our resources.

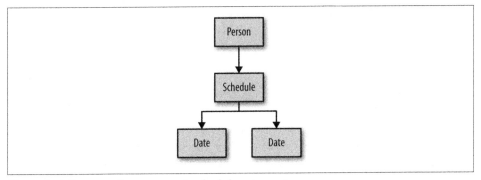

Figure 1-4. Representing a person's schedule using actors

Uses of the Actor Model

The Actor Model is a powerful tool, and when applied carefully, can be effective at providing highly scalable, highly concurrent applications. But like any tool, it is not perfect. If you apply it incorrectly, the Actor Model can be just as likely to create complex code that is difficult to follow and even more difficult to debug. After you learn the tools, you might decide that you want to apply the Actor Model at all levels of your application, creating a true Actor System. But early on, it is sometimes safer to just get your feet wet and ease into it. In later chapters, we will explore these ideas further and provide additional guidelines about what an individual actor should be modeling.

One thing to realize about the Actor Model is that, like other techniques, there are times when you might want to apply it, but there are other times when you might not. You might find that in certain cases an alternative model is more suitable for the task at hand. And in those cases, you should not be afraid to use those tools or techniques. The Actor Model is not an all-or-nothing proposition. The key is to figure out where you need it and where you don't, and then create a clear and distinct line separating the two.

Defining Clear Boundaries

Many successful systems are modeled with actors representing top-level entities in the system, and then using a more functional approach within those actors. There is nothing wrong with this approach. In addition, it is common to see a small group of actors wrapped within an a interface such that clients of that interface aren't aware that they are communicating with actors. Again, this is a good approach. Both create clear boundaries. In the first case, you have actors only at the top level. All of the implementation is done by using functional programming. In the second case, the interface creates a boundary between what are actors and what are not.

If you have decided to use the Actor Model for a portion of your application, you should stick to the model throughout that section. You should only break from the model on clearly defined boundaries. These boundaries could be the boundary between your frontend and backend services. Or, it could be the boundary between two different microservices in your application. There are many ways in which to partition your application and many ways to apply the Actor Model. You should, however, avoid breaking the Actor Model mid context. One of the things that contributes to messy, complex code is when the code transitions between styles with no clear pattern or explanation as to why the transition has occurred. You don't want to find yourself in a situation in which you jump into and out of the Actor Model multiple times within a single context. Instead, look to break from the model along consistency boundaries or domain boundaries.

Let's consider a concrete example. In our scheduling domain, we might want to build a library to handle the scheduling. Within that library, we would prefer to use the Actor Model, but outside the boundaries of the library we want to use other techniques. This is a good example of a system boundary where it is OK to transition from one model of computation to another.

One way to handle this would be to expose everything as actors. The external client code would be fully aware that it is interfacing with actors. Thus, we might have a message protocol that looks something like this:

```
object ProjectProtocol {
  case class ScheduleProject(project: Project)
  case class ProjectScheduled(project: Project)
}
```

Using this code within the client would mean sending a message along the lines of this:

```
def scheduleProject(details: ProjectDetails): Future[Project] = {

  val project = createProject(details)

  val result = (projects ? ProjectProtocol.ScheduleProject(project))
    .mapTo[ProjectProtocol.ProjectScheduled]
    .map(_.project)

  result
}
```

This is OK, but it's not great. The problem here is that we have actor code interspersed with other code. This other code might have different concurrency mechanisms. There can actually be several steps in this process. You might first need to create a project, and then schedule the project and potentially perform other operations, as well. Each of these can involve going to the scheduling system, which means interfacing with actors. Yet there might be other parts of the code that communicate with other contexts that don't use actors, so there can be function calls and futures and other mechanisms here, as well. This constant jumping in and out of the Actor Model can become difficult to follow when it's not well isolated. A better approach in this case is to create a wrapper API over the top of your actors, as demonstrated here:

```
class ProjectApi(projects: ActorRef) {
    def scheduleProject(project: Project): Future[Project] = {
        val result = (projects ? ProjectProtocol.ScheduleProject(project))
          .mapTo[ProjectProtocol.ProjectScheduled]
          .map(_.project)
    }
}
```

This thin wrapper around the actors provides the insulation layer. It gives us a clear transitional boundary between what are actors and what are not. Now, when we want to use this API, it looks like the following:

```
def scheduleProject(details: ProjectDetails): Future[Project] = {

  val project = createProject(details)

  val result = projectApi.scheduleProject(project)

  result
}
```

The code is shorter, but really we have just moved any complexity within a separate function. So is that really better? The advantage of this approach is that the client code doesn't need to be aware that actors are being used internally. Actors in this case have become an implementation detail rather than an intrinsic part of the API. Now when we use this API, we are taking advantage of it using function calls, which means when we nest them alongside other function calls, everything looks more consistent and more clean. As the code base grows, and the actors become more complex, this kind of isolation can be critical to keeping the system maintainable.

Should we do this everywhere? Should all actors have an API wrapper around them so that the application never needs to know that it is dealing with actors? The simple answer is "no." Within our scheduling library, which is built using the Actor Model, this kind of wrapper interface is not only unnecessary, it creates unwanted complexity. It actually makes it more difficult to work with the actors within the actor system. When we're using the Actor Model we should be dealing with actors, and we should not be trying to hide that fact. It's only on the boundaries of the system—where we want to transition to a different model—that we should be creating this kind of isolation.

When Is the Actor Model Appropriate?

We have decided that there are times to use actors by themselves and other times for which we might use the full Actor Model. And we know that when we use them, we need to be careful to do so within a clearly defined context. But when is the right time to use them? When should we use standalone actors and when should we build a full-fledged actor system? Of course, it is impossible to say you should always use one or the other in a certain situation. Each situation is unique. Still, there are some guidelines that you might take into account when making the decision.

The first obvious candidate for using actors is when you have a high degree of concurrency and you need to maintain some sort of state. Maintaining concurrent state is the bread and butter of the Actor Model.

Another obvious case for actors and the Actor Model is when you're modeling finite-state machines, as an actor is a very natural construct for this task. Again, if you are limited to only a single finite-state machine, a single actor might do the job, but if you are going to have multiple machines, possibly interacting with one another, the Actor Model should be considered.

A more subtle case that might suit actors is when you need a high degree of concurrency, but you need to be careful in how that concurrency is managed. For example, you might need to ensure that a specific set of operations can run concurrently with other operations within your system, but also that they cannot operate concurrently with one another. In our scheduling example, this might mean that you want multiple users to be able to concurrently modify projects in the system, but you don't want those users to be able to modify the same project at the same time. This is an opportunity to use the single-threaded illusion provided by actors to your advantage. The users can all operate independently, but you can funnel any changes to a particular project through an actor associated with that project.

Conclusion

As you can see, the Actor Model is indeed a powerful tool, and like all powerful tools, you need to understand and carefully control it to gain the most advantage from it. You should not blindly run into every problem assuming that the Actor Model will always be the best fit. Still, after you have a solid understanding of it—and how and when to apply it—you will find that it can in fact be applied to a wide variety of cases. Because it naturally reflects the asynchronous nature of the real world, it is an excellent tool for modeling a broad range of circumstances. After you master it, you can shake loose the shackles of global consistency and begin to understand that nothing happens instantly and everything is relative to the observer.

The Actor Model is a different paradigm for organizing your application functionality, with many advantages. The foundation we laid in this chapter will be extended in the remainder of this book to show you how to build good actors and take full advantage of the power of the model.

As you continue, however, keep in mind that many elements of the Actor Model will seem unusual and restrictive at first. There are good reasons for such restrictions, and the power of the model more than makes up for the initial effort to fully master it.

CHAPTER 2

Introducing Akka

In this chapter, we introduce Akka, the open source library we use throughout the remainder of this book. If you're reading this far, you probably already have a good idea about what Akka is, but you might not know the whole story.

Akka is a toolkit that you can use to implement all of the patterns we discuss in the remainder of the book, allowing you to put these techniques to immediate and practical use in your own applications.

What Is Akka?

Akka is described on its home page as "an open source toolkit and runtime simplifying the construction of concurrent and distributed applications on the Java Virtual Machine (JVM)."

It goes on to say that Akka supports multiple programming models but emphasizes actor-based concurrency, with inspiration drawn from Erlang.

This is a good high-level description, but Akka is much more. Let's look a bit deeper.

Akka Is Open Source

Akka is an open source project released under the Apache 2 License, a recognized open source license, making it free to use and extend in both other open source efforts and in commercial libraries and applications.

Although it is fully usable from Java, Akka is itself written in Scala and gains the benefit of the attributes of this language as a result, including strong type safety, high performance, low memory footprint, and compatibility with all other JVM libraries and languages. One of the key features of the Scala language that is used heavily in Akka is the focus on immutable data structures. Akka makes heavy use of them in its messaging protocols. In fact, it is not uncommon to see Java users write their messages in Scala in order to save time.

There are even adapter toolkits to use Akka from Clojure, an implementation of Lisp on the JVM.

Akka Is Under Active Development

Akka is continually being developed, and usually no more than a few months go by without at least a minor release. The ecosystem of libraries and contributed add-ons is even more active.

There are concerted efforts underway to create versions of Akka for the .NET platform and for JavaScript.

Akka moves fairly rapidly but continues to support stable versions for a long period. The upgrade path from one major version to the next has historically been quite smooth, allowing projects that use Akka to upgrade regularly with minimal risk.

Akka Is Distributed by Design

Akka, like many other implementations of the Actor Model, doesn't only target multi-core, single computer systems—you can also use it with clusters of systems. It is, therefore, designed to present the same programming model for both local and distributed development—virtually nothing changes in the way you develop your code when deploying across many systems, making it easy to develop and test locally and then deploy distributed.

With Akka, it is natural to model interactions as messages, as opposed to systems such as Remote Procedure Call (RPC), for which it is more natural to model interactions as procedure calls. This is an important distinction, as we will see in detail later.

Although it is possible to write code that is aware of the distributed nature of the cluster (e.g., by listening to events as nodes join and leave the cluster), the actual logic within the actors themselves does not change. Whether dealing with local actors or remote, the communication mechanisms, delivery guarantees, failure handling, and other concepts remain unchanged.

Akka provides a key element in the construction of so-called *Reactive* applications; that is, applications built to support the fundamental attributes discussed in the Reactive Manifesto (which you can see at *http://www.reactivemanifesto.org/*). The manifesto describes applications that are *responsive, resilient, elastic,* and *message driven*. The message-driven part is where Akka comes in, and through its capabilities, supports the rest of the attributes.

In an Akka system, an actor can be *local* or *remote*. It is local with respect to any other actor if the sending and receiving actors are in the same JVM.

If an actor is determined to be local, Akka can make certain optimizations in delivery (no serialization or network call is required), but the code is no different than if the receiving actor were remote.

That's what we mean by "distributed by design": no code changes between local operation and distributed operation.

Akka Components

Akka consists of not only the core of Akka itself, but of a rich set of optional additional libraries that work with it, so you can customize the portions you use in your project. Most of the Akka components are open source, but there are also commercial add-ons available.

Lightbend provides commercial support and indemnification for Akka as well as for the rest of its reactive platform, and many organizations provide development and consulting services around Akka. This commercial ecosystem further lessens the risk for organizations adopting it, while at the same time not limiting the hobbyist or developer who wants to use Akka on his own.

Akka Actor

The primary component of the Akka library is the implementation of actors themselves, which are the fundamental building block on which Akka is built. All of the attributes of the Actor Model are supplied here, but only on a single JVM—distributed and clustering support are optional components.

Akka actors implement the Actor Model with no shared state and asynchronous message passing. They also support a sophisticated error-handling hierarchy, which we'll dig into later.

The Akka API intentionally limits the access to an actor. Communication between actors can happen only through message passing. There is no way to call methods in the actor in a synchronous fashion, so actors remain decoupled from one another both in API and in time. It does this through the use of an `ActorRef`. When an an instance of an actor is created, only an `ActorRef` is returned. The `ActorRef` is a wrapper around the actual actor. It isolates that actor from the rest of the code. All communication with the actor must go through the `ActorRef`, and the `ActorRef` does not provide any access to the actor that it wraps.

This means that unlike regular object-oriented method calls, whereby the caller blocks, passes control to the called object, and then resumes when the called object returns, the messages to an actor are sent via the `ActorRef`, and the caller continues immediately. The receiving actor then processes the messages that were sent to it one at a time, likely on a completely different thread from the caller. The fact that messages are processed one at a time is what enables the single-threaded illusion. While inside of an Akka actor, we can be confident that only a single thread will be modifying the state of that actor, as long as we don't actively break the single-threaded illusion. Later we will discuss ways by which we can break the single-threaded illusion, and why that should be avoided.

The message-driven nature of the Actor Model is implemented in Akka through the ActorRef. An ActorRef provides a number of methods that allow us to send messages to the underlying actor. Those messages typically take the form of immutable case classes. Even though there is nothing preventing us from sending mutable messages to an actor, it is considered a bad practice because it is one way that we can break the single-threaded illusion.

Changes in the behavior of an actor in Akka are implemented through the use of become. Any actor can call context.become to provide a new behavior for the next message. You also can use this technique to change an actor's state. However, actors can also maintain and change state by using mutable fields and class parameters. We will discuss techniques for changing state and behavior in more detail later.

Child Actors

Akka actors also can create child actors. There are various factory methods available within an actor that allows it to create those children. Any actor in the system will have access to its parent and children and can freely send messages to those other actors. This is also what enables the supervision mechanism in Akka because parent actors will automatically supervise their children.

The supervision mechanism in Akka means that this message-passing structure can focus on the "happy path," because errors have an entirely separate path through which to propagate.

When an actor encounters an error, the caller is not aware of it—after all, the caller could be long gone or on another machine entirely, so sending it the error isn't necessarily helpful. Instead, Akka passes errors from an actor to its *supervisor* actor; that is, the actor that started it in the first place. Those supervisor actors then use a special method to handle those exceptions, and to inform the actor that threw the exception as to what to do next—to ignore the error or to restart (with various options).

This is the origin of the "let it crash" saying that is associated with Akka; in other words, the idea is that it is acceptable for the actor that had the problem to simply "crash." We don't try to prevent the failure of the actor. Instead, we handle it appropriately when it happens. If an actor crashes, we can take certain actions to recover that actor. This can include stopping the actor, ignoring the failure and continuing with message processing, or it can even mean restarting the actor. When an actor is restarted, we transparently replace it with a new copy of that actor. Because communication is handled through the `ActorRef`, the clients of the actor need not be aware that the actor failed. From their perspective, nothing has changed. They continue to point to the same `ActorRef`, but the actor that supports it has been replaced. This keeps the overall system resilient because the error is isolated to the failing actor. It need not propagate any further.

Figure 2-1 shows three actors in a single actor system within a single JVM. Any actor can send messages to any other, in both directions (although we only show two possible routes).

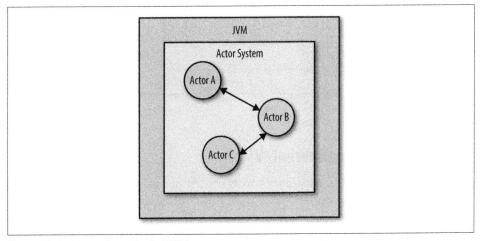

Figure 2-1. Actors in a single JVM

In addition to the usual message-passing mechanism of actors, which is point-to-point, Akka also provides a one-to-many messaging mechanism, called the *event bus*. The event bus allows a single actor to *publish* a message, and other actors to *subscribe* to that message by its type. The sending actor then remains completely decoupled from the receiver, which is very valuable in some situations.

Note that the event bus is optimized only for local messaging; when using Akka in a distributed environment, the publish/subscribe module provides equivalent functionality optimized for multiple nodes.

Figure 2-2 shows the three actors again, but this time, instead of communicating directly with one another, they communicate bidirectionally with the event bus, improving decoupling.

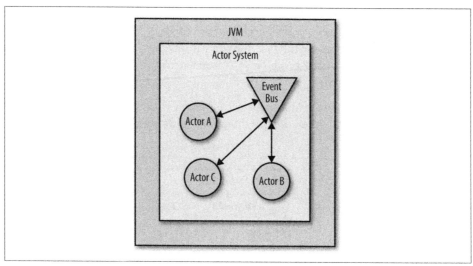

Figure 2-2. Actors and event bus

Remoting: Actors on Different JVMs

Akka provides location transparency for its actors; that is, when you have an actor reference to which you can send messages, you don't actually need to know if that actor is on the local system or on another machine altogether.

Remoting provides the ability for the actor system to communicate over a network, and to serialize and deserialize messages so that actors on different JVMs can pass messages to one another.

This is enabled in part through the actor's unique address. An actor's address can include not only the unique path to the actor in the hierarchy, but also a network address for that actor. This network address means that we can uniquely identify any actor in any actor system, even when that actor resides in a different JVM running on a different machine. Because we have access to that address, we can use it to send messages to the remote actor as though it were a local actor. The Akka platform will take care of the delivery mechanics for us, including serializing and sending the message.

The serialization mechanism is pluggable, as is the communication protocol, so a number of choices are available. When starting out, the default mechanisms are often sufficient, but as your application grows, you might want to consider swapping in different serializers or communication protocols.

Remoting in Akka can be added by configuration only: no code changes are necessary, although it is also possible to write code to explicitly perform remoting.

With remoting, each node must be *aware* of the other nodes and must have their network address because the messaging is point-to-point and explicit. Akka Remoting does not include any discovery mechanisms. Those come as part of Akka clustering.

Clustering: Automatic Management of Membership

For larger groups of servers, remoting becomes awkward: adding a node to a group means that every other node in the group must be informed, and message routing can grow pretty complex.

Akka provides the *clustering* module to help simplify this process.

Akka clustering offers additional capabilities on top of Remoting that make it easier to provide for location-independence. Clustering provides the ability for actor systems running in multiple JVMs to interact with one another and behave as though they are part of the same actor system. These systems form a single, cohesive clustered actor system.

Akka clustering makes the location-transparency of actors much more accessible. Before clustering, you needed at least some part of your code to be aware of the location of remote actors, and you needed to build addresses for those actors to send messages to them. Failover was more difficult to manage: if the node you were communicating with for your remote actors became unavailable or failed, you needed to handle starting up another node and creating connections to the new actors on that node yourself.

With Akka clustering, instead of one node needing to be aware of other nodes on the network directly, it needs to be aware of only one or more *seed nodes*. These are specially designated nodes that can be used to connect to the cluster by new nodes that are looking to join.

You can (but probably shouldn't) have a single seed node in your cluster, or you can designate every node as a possible seed. The idea is that as long as one of the seed nodes is available, new nodes can join the cluster.

No special code is required: configuration informs your actor system as to where the seed nodes are, and it contacts one of them automatically on startup.

The new node then goes through a series of lifecycle steps (as seen in Figure 2-3) until it is a full member of the cluster, at which point it is not only capable of sending messages to other actors in the cluster, it can also start new actors, either in its own actor system or on another node of the cluster. In essence, the cluster becomes a single virtual actor system.

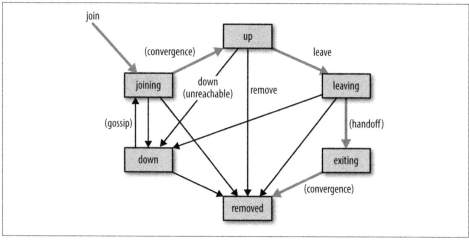

Figure 2-3. Cluster states

Although the actors within the cluster can send messages to one another, the cluster management itself is handled separately. A variant of the *gossip* protocol is used by the actor system itself to manage cluster membership. Random peers communicate what information they have about cluster membership to another node—that node passes on what it knows to another, and so on. After a time, *convergence* occurs. Convergence is when all nodes get a cohesive picture of the membership of the cluster (and all have the same version of the cluster information structure), yet there is no one central node that contains this information. It is a robust and resilient system, used in many other distributed applications such as Amazon's Dynamo (*http://amzn.to/2gW7rVW*) and Basho's Riak (*http://basho.com/products/*). *Vector clocks*, which do not actually track wall-clock time, but are a way of determining a partial ordering of events in a distributed system, are used to reconcile messages received via the gossip protocol into an accurate state of the cluster.

Special event messages are sent automatically as cluster lifecycle events occur—for instance, a new node joining, or an existing node leaving the cluster. You do not *need* to listen to these events to use the cluster, but if you want more fine-grained control or monitoring, you can.

For nodes determined to be missing from the cluster, a Phi Accrual failure detector is used to determine when a node has become *unreachable*, and eventually, that the node is *down*. The cluster supports a heartbeat to support this detection. Of course, a node can leave the cluster intentionally, as well—for instance, during a controlled downscaling or shutdown.

For a description of the Phi Accrual failure detection method, check out the paper "The φ Accrual Failure Detector" (*http://bit.ly/phi-accrual*).

Cluster leader

Each cluster has a *leader*. Every node can determine algorithmically which node should be the current leader based on the information supplied by gossip; it is not necessary that the leader be elected. The leader, however, is not a point of failure, because a new leader can be established by any node as necessity arises. It is also not especially relevant to developers, because the leader is used only internally by Akka to make certain cluster-related decisions.

The leader does two things for the cluster: it adds new members to the cluster when they become eligible to be added, and it takes them out when appropriate. It also schedules the *rebalancing* of the cluster as necessary; that is, the movement of actors between members of the cluster. Because the leader has limited duties, the cluster can continue to function even in the absence of a leader. In this case, all traffic among cluster nodes can continue as before; it is only the changes to the cluster that will be delayed until a new leader is established. You will not be able to add or remove nodes from the cluster, but it can still perform all of its other duties despite the absence.

A potential issue with distributed systems is the issue of *partitioning*. In a cluster, if a node terminates unexpectedly, other nodes simply take over its function, and all is well. However, if a group of nodes is suddenly disconnected from the cluster—say, due to a network failure—but does *not* terminate, an issue can arise. The surviving nodes carry on, but who are the survivors? Each group of nodes, now isolated from the others, can potentially form a new cluster, leading to a situation called *split-brain*, in which there should only be one cluster but there are in fact two. In this situation, guarantees such as the uniqueness of a cluster singleton can be compromised.

There are several techniques to deal with this situation. The simplest is to disallow autodowning. When autodowning is enabled, if a node becomes unreachable, the system will automatically remove it from the cluster after a period of time. This seems like a good thing on paper, but in practice this is what leads to difficulties. It leads to the split-brain. One or more downed nodes can form their own cluster, giving rise to the problem. By disabling autodowning, this is no longer possible. Now, when nodes become unreachable, human intervention is required in order to remove the node from the cluster. In this way, new clusters can't form, because it is impossible to reach the critical convergence required. Generally, autodowning should not be enabled in production.

However, if autodowning is used, there are still other options. It is possible to restrict the minimum size of a cluster (this is something you can configure). In this case, if a single node is disconnected, it cannot form a cluster, because it doesn't have enough members, so it terminates. Picking the right minimum value is situational, though: there's no one right answer.

Lightbend also provides a smart *split-brain resolver* product as a commercial add-on that helps in this situation. It uses more sophisticated techniques to determine if a cluster partition has occurred and then takes appropriate action.

Cluster sharding

The idea of *sharding* was initially applied to databases, for which a single set of data could grow to be too large to fit in a single node. To spread the data more or less evenly across multiple nodes, the idea of a *shard key* was defined: some value that was part of the data that had a good, wide distribution. This shard key could be used to chop up the data set into a number of smaller parts.

Akka cluster sharding takes this further by applying the principles of sharding to live actors, allowing them to be distributed across a cluster.

An example of a shard key might be the first letter of the last name of a customer: you could then break up your data into a maximum of 26 *shards*, wherein shard 1 would have the data for all customers with last names beginning with "A," for instance.

In practice, this is a terrible shard key, but it's a simple illustration.

As you begin to add more nodes to your Akka cluster, the number of actors that are available grows substantially, in many cases, and you can apply cluster sharding in much the same manner as you would apply it to a database.

Akka cluster sharding takes the concept of sharding and extends it so that you can shard live actors across a cluster.

Each node can be assigned to a shard *region*, and there can be (and probably should be) more than one node assigned to each region.

Messages that are intended for use in a cluster-sharded environment are then wrapped in a special envelope that includes a value that can be used to determine the shard region to which that message should be delivered. All messages that resolve to that shard region are delivered only to that region, allowing for state contained in those actors to be stored only on those nodes.

In the previous, simple example, if you have a shard region for all customers whose last names begin with "A," the value of the customer's last name can be used to resolve to the shard region, and the message will be delivered to the correct node(s).

Distributed domains with cluster sharding

One of the significant advantages of cluster sharding is that persistence for the state of the actors within a region can be restricted to the shard region nodes—it need not be replicated or shared across the entire cluster. For instance, suppose that you're keeping an account balance for customers. You can persist this balance by storing every message that changes the balance and then save this journal to disk. In this way, when the actor that encapsulates this state is restarted, it can just read the journal and be back at the correct balance.

With the capabilities of Akka clustering and cluster sharding, it is possible to build a system that uses what has been called a *distributed domain*. This is the technique of having a single actor holding state for an instance of a domain (say, a customer) somewhere in a cluster-sharded actor system. We will explore this pattern in some depth later in this book.

If the actor in question is for a customer whose last name begins with "A," its journal need be kept only on the nodes in that shard region—because we can guarantee that the actor for that customer starts up *only* on one of those nodes—as opposed to the usual cluster situation, in which an actor can be started anywhere in the cluster. You need to take care when applying this technique, however, because it restricts the flexibility of the cluster significantly.

Cluster singleton

Another refinement in clustering is the *cluster singleton*—that is, a specific actor that must always have one, and *exactly* one, instance in the cluster. It doesn't matter where it is in the cluster, but it's important that there is just the one.

In this case, Akka provides a special means to ensure this: each node is capable of starting the singleton, but only one node can do so at a time. If that actor for some reason fails, the same or another node will start it back up again, ensuring that it remains available as much as possible. Every node that needs to send messages to the singleton has a *proxy*, which routes messages to the singleton no matter where it is in the cluster.

Of course, like any singleton, there are disadvantages, but the failover mechanism takes away at least one of them. You can still end up with a performance bottleneck, however, so you must use cluster singletons with care.

Akka HTTP

Inspired by the Spray HTTP library, Akka HTTP replaces it while providing a deeper integration with Akka and Akka Streams. It provides a way to build HTTP APIs on top of Akka and is the recommended approach for interfacing Akka with other HTTP-based systems.

TestKit

Core to any good toolkit is the ability to test the code you produce with it, and Akka is no exception. Asynchronous and concurrent programs are notoriously difficult to test, but the facilities that TestKit provides allow you to verify functionality easily and completely, and even to write your code test-first if you choose to do so, with none of the normal difficulties of asynchronous development.

TestKit overcomes one of the most intractable problems with either concurrency or with distribution: how can you test such a system repeatedly and reliably?

The nature of concurrent execution brings with it the difficulty that the exact order of operations is in fact unknown. The same is true of distributed systems, which are, of course, also concurrent but with the added complexity that more than one physical system is involved, introducing elements such as networking and serialization/deserialization into the testing equation.

The TestKit enables this in two ways. The simplest is providing a way to test an actor that temporarily—for the scope of the test—allows access to the actor in a fully synchronous and deterministic fashion. This makes an actor no more difficult to test than any other code. However, it has the potential to hide or even create problems. A fully synchronous and deterministic actor does not represent the real world. It could change the behavior of the actor in ways that allow the test to pass or fail when they might behave otherwise had the actor remained asynchronous.

The second capability that TestKit brings to testing is a means to verify messages sent and received between actors in their normal nondeterministic and asynchronous modes: it does this by providing an easy way to stub or fake actors, along with methods to assert that certain messages have been received within specific timeout periods, without the need to specify in what order the actual operations occurred.

A final add-on, which is not specifically a part of the Akka TestKit, but works very well with it, is the multi-JVM test. This is a means for a single test to launch an entirely new instance of the JVM, simulating a network of nodes and allowing interaction between the isolated actor systems to be verified. This feature was developed by the Akka team to test actors in close-to-production setups, across multiple virtual machines (VMs), and even multiple physical nodes.

Contrib

A library called "contrib" is available for Akka, which contains many different contributed tools that have not made their way into their own top-level modules yet. This includes useful tools for throttling messages, aggregating them, and more. It is worth exploring, with many uncut gems inside.

Akka OSGi

The OSGi model has much to recommend it as a host environment for Akka, and specific support is provided by this module, which allows the OSGi lifecycle to initialize the actor system of modules with Akka support at the right time.

Akka HTTP

Akka HTTP provides the recommended way to expose actors as REST endpoints, and build RESTful web services.

Akka Streams

Akka Streams provides a higher-level API for interacting with actors while at the same time providing automatic handling of "back pressure" (which we will discuss in detail later on).

Streams provides a way of building complex structures called streams and graphs that are based on actors. You can use these structures to consume and transform data via a convenient and familiar domain-specific language (DSL).

These streams follow the Reactive Streams initiative.

Akka's Implementation of the Actor Model

We have said that Akka provides the Actor Model (and a few other things) on the JVM. Let's examine that a bit more closely, and see how Akka gives us the attributes of the Actor Model specifically.

Akka's Actors in the Actor Model

The fundamental unit of computation in the Actor Model is the actor, and Akka provides this directly, with a number of traits that provide actors and specializations of actors. In an upcoming version of Akka, typed actors will in fact remove the trait called "Actor," but will replace it with traits specific to defining the behavior of actors, which results in the same thing, semantically.

Actors in Akka are where the computation occurs, as prescribed by Hewitt.

A simple actor looks like this:

```
import akka.actor.Actor

class DemoActor extends Actor {
  def receive = {
    case _ => println("Received a message")
  }
}
```

Message Passing

The Actor Model specifies that message passing should be the only way for actors to communicate, and that all processing should occur in response to this message passing.

In Akka, messages are the only means for actors to interact with one another and the outside world. Messages are passed to other actors via a nonblocking queue called the mailbox. The object reference of the actor itself is not used directly—only an intermediary called the `ActorRef`, (for Actor Reference). This queue is normally first-in/first-out, but can take other forms if desired.

There are three message-passing mechanisms in Akka, to be precise. Let's take a look at each one.

Tell

The preferred mechanism for sending messages is the *tell*, sometimes called "bang," based on the name of the shorthand for the method, "!".

You specify a "tell" by using the "!" operator, like this:

```
projectsActor ! List
```

Which is the equivalent of

```
projectsActor.tell(List)
```

(Let's assume that List is a case object here.)

The tell method is the classic "fire and forget" message in the Actor Model: it neither blocks nor waits for any response.

Ask

You need to use caution when using the ask method because it is easy to write blocking code that will significantly reduce the advantages of an asynchronous system with *ask*.

The shorthand for ask is "?", as demonstrated here:

```
projectsActor ? List
```

An ask indicates that a response is expected. The response is captured in a future because the actor to which the ask is sent might not respond immediately.

Publish/subscribe

The final means of message sending in Akka is via the event bus, described previously. The sender of a message uses a reference to the event bus to *publish* a message.

A receiver of the message must independently *subscribe* to the type of the message, and will therefore receive every message of that type that another actor publishes. The two actors are not directly aware of each other, and no *sender* reference is available for a message received this way.

Actor Systems

A single actor is no actor at all, according to the Actor Model. Akka provides the concept of actor *systems*; that is, groups of actors that are able to exchange messages readily, whether they are running in a single JVM or across many.

Although it is possible for actors in different actor systems to communicate, it is not common.

An actor system also serves as the facility to create or locate actors, like so:

```
import akka.actor.{Actor, ActorSystem, Props}

val system = ActorSystem("demo")

val actor = system.actorOf(Props[DemoActor])
```

Creating new actors

Actors in Akka can be created both from outside the system, as well as by other actors, satisfying Hewitt's requirement that new actors can create "child" actors.

Changing behavior

Actors in Akka have the ability to swap out the behavior that they use to respond to messages with another behavior, which can handle perhaps a completely different set of messages. Akka does this with the become and unbecome operations with untyped actors. Akka Typed, a future version of actors that we will explore in more detail in just a moment, returns the behavior for handling the next message after every message is handled.

Akka goes a step further and supplies a convenient DSL for creating finite-state machine actors specifically, a common use case for changing behavior.

The Akka Typed Project

In Akka 2.4, an experimental project has been added to the main Akka distribution: Akka Typed.

This project is actually the latest in a series of efforts to reconcile the strongly typed nature of Scala with the nature of actor receive methods. Currently, you can think of a receive method as a partial function that takes any type and returns a unit, in essence.

This is because any message class can be sent to any actor—nothing in the type system stops this, although many custom attempts have been made to introduce type constraints.

Akka Typed starts from a simple premise: an actor is all about its *behavior*, and that behavior can have a type. That type indicates the set of messages that are valid to be handled by that behavior, and no others can be handled. Thus, why not have the compiler prevent them from being sent in the first place?

Akka Typed also eliminates the Actor trait itself, instead supplying a few types to directly declare behaviors and the types of the messages they accept.

Instead of lifecycle methods, Akka Typed follows the Actor Model even more strictly: lifecycle events are represented by messages, instead.

In this new version of Akka, the entire actor system is typed, as well. Creating an actor system provides a constructor that takes a Props object for the top-level actor.

Akka Typed is still experimental, but shows great promise.

Conclusion

Akka is a rich implementation of the Actor Model designed to work with your existing JVM languages, allowing you to take full advantage of actors from the languages you already use.

If you weren't already using a JVM-based language, however, the opportunity to work with the huge and mature ecosystem of libraries available on the JVM still makes Akka an attractive option.

Now we have introduced both the model and the implementation of that model that we will use for the remainder of our discussions. In Chapter 3, we will start discussing the architecture and design approaches that can allow you to make full use of actors with Akka.

Distributed Domain-Driven Design

As you explore the tools and techniques that Akka offers, you will find a need for something to tie all of the concepts together. You need a guiding set of principles that will help you design not just your actors, but also the larger components that make up an entire system. As you learn about new concepts like clustering, it will become apparent that you need a way to divide your application into smaller subsystems. You need to understand the boundaries for those subsystems and how they interact. The guiding principles we will use for this come from domain-driven design (DDD). When put together in a distributed Akka system, we will use the term distributed domain-driven design (DDDD).

DDD is a widely adopted concept initially created by Eric Evans. We will be covering some of the basics, but if you are interested in pursuing DDD further, you should look for Evans' original book[1] or some of the follow-up books by people like Vaughn Vernon.[2]

DDD Overview

DDD is a set of guiding principles for software architecture. The principles of DDD are not revolutionary. In fact, a common reaction to people hearing them for the first time is "well, of course. That's obvious." It is not the principles themselves that are so powerful; rather, it's how they are applied and how they are combined. Applying them consistently throughout a project can transform that project from something that is cumbersome and awkward into one that is elegant and considerably more useful.

---

[1] Evans, Eric. *Domain-Driven Design: Tackling Complexity in the Heart of Software*. Boston: Addison-Wesley, 2003.

[2] Vernon, Vaughn. *Implementing Domain-Driven Design*. Boston: Addison-Wesley, 2013.

The most important concept in DDD is the focus on the Domain Model. If you are not familiar with the term "domain," it is the set of requirements, constraints, and concepts that make up the business or field that you are trying to model. In DDD, we focus on that business domain and we model our software around it. We are trying to model our software in a way that reflects the real world and how it operates. We want our model to capture the truth of the domain that we are trying to model. This involves conversations with domain experts. These experts are people who are knowledgeable about the domain but might not be technically savvy. They can include lawyers, marketing staff, support staff, business managers, or anyone else with a knowledge of the domain. This means that it is important to use language that makes sense to those experts, not just in our conversations, but also in our code. This language that we develop is shared between the developers and the domain experts and is called the *ubiquitous language*.

When we establish a ubiquitous language, it eases our ability to communicate about the software, not just among developers but with the domain experts, as well. It allows us to have a conversation about the software, referring to actions and objects within the application in a way that is still intelligible to nondevelopers. This in turn helps the domain experts feel involved in the software in a way that would otherwise be impossible. When you begin explaining the model using their language, they are able to point out flaws in the way that you are using that language. Those flaws will often be reflected as deficiencies in the developer's understanding of the domain that will have crept into the software itself. Being able to speak in this common language is an invaluable tool in the development process.

This common language can change meaning from one area of the domain to another. The individual concepts, what actions are available, and how they interact within the domain might not always be the same. Each concept is bound within a particular context. Within that context, the language has a certain meaning. When we leave that context and move to another area of the domain, the meaning can change.

A key part of this is recognizing that the domain is not fixed. It is a fluid entity that can change over time. Sometimes, the rules of the business change. Sometimes, our understanding of those rules evolves. We need to be prepared for those changes and we need to be prepared to adapt the Domain Model to accommodate the changes. If we build a model expecting it to handle all cases and to never change, we are doomed to failure.

DDD focuses on building models that are equipped to evolve. We don't build a model the first time and expect it to last. We build it with the understanding that it will fail at some point and we will need to adapt. Accordingly, we need to build it in a way that allows it to adapt. The cost of change must remain small. DDD gives us a set of tools to help keep that cost of change low.

The Benefits of DDD

One of the worst ways that you can cripple your software and prevent it from evolving is by creating too much coupling between areas of the system that are conceptually different. In particular, when you create coupling between portions of an application that are considered part of the domain and portions that are considered part of the infrastructure, you reduce your ability to adapt. DDD helps to distinguish what is domain and what is infrastructure, but it also helps to create the right abstractions around them so that you don't violate those boundaries.

Let's consider a very simple example. Suppose that your company has been using a particular email library for years. This library has been working well, but now a new web-based service has come onto the scene that has the business owners excited. This new service provides all sorts of tracking tools that were previously unavailable. It will give you great metrics and a great view into your customers. The business owners ask that you convert the system to use this new email service.

You begin digging into the code and we realize how difficult of a problem this is. The old email library has been forcibly integrated into the code. There are hooks everywhere. If you want to convert to using this new system, you need to begin modifying the application in many different areas. The scheduling engine uses emails for notifications; it needs to change. The user management system uses emails for sending out confirmation emails and invitations, so it needs to change, too. There are even emails being triggered by a stored procedure within your database. Where does it end?

DDD introduces a number of concepts that help solve problems like this. It helps you to recognize that the concerns about how emails are sent are not part of the domain of user management or of the decision engine. It's an infrastructure concern. The scheduling engine needs to send notifications, not emails. The fact that those notifications are delivered via email is not relevant. It is certainly not relevant that those emails be sent with a specific version of a particular library.

Recognizing the differences in the language being used (notification versus email) is only the first step. You also need to be able to recognize that how you manage users and make decisions about those users might be entirely different. It might be difficult or impossible to create a single model that captures all the needs of both.

The goal with DDD is to decompose the larger domain into smaller, easier-to-manage chunks. You can then model those chunks individually, and in doing so, you can develop a better understanding not just for yourself, but for the domain experts, as well. You can go back to the domain experts and talk about sending notifications within the scheduling engine. Sure, we are talking about emails, but by using the correct term of "notification," you can prepare for the possibility that at some point this might become a text message, or a social media message, or whatever the next big thing happens to be. You can also talk to those domain experts specifically about sending emails and what is involved there, and you don't need to blend your concerns. We don't need your infrastructure to leak into the domain.

Components of DDD

So, what are the tools that help you to decompose the application using DDD? More importantly, how are those tools related to Akka?

DDD provides a set of tools that you can apply directly in the code. These are your building blocks. But in addition to the smaller building blocks there are higher level concepts that help us understand how to take the pieces that we build with those small blocks and combine them to create even larger software systems.

Often these building blocks are perfect candidates for determining the right structure for your actors. When trying to decide whether a particular concept deserves a new actor or should be rolled into an existing one, you can use the building blocks of DDD to help make that determination. Many of these building blocks have natural parallels within Akka, so it can be very easy to simply map the domain concepts directly into the Actor Model.

Let's begin by looking at some of the smaller pieces.

Domain Entities

DDD uses the concept of an Entity to refer to objects in the system that are uniquely identifiable by a key or composite key. Entities can be mutable. That is, if an Entity changes its state in some way but its key remains unaffected, it is considered to be the same Entity—its identity has not changed.

The nature of Entities, the fact that they can contain mutable state and are uniquely identifiable, maps directly to Akka actors. Actors are all about managing mutable state. And every actor in the system is uniquely identifiable using its path, regardless of the data that actor contains. It is therefore natural for us to use actors in our system the same way we might use Entities in a nonactor-based system. You can treat them as equivalent.

For example, if your system has a user Entity, you could model that user as an actor:

```
class User(id: UUID) extends Actor {
  override def receive: Receive = ...
}
```

When our User actor receives messages, the actor's internal state may change. But the path to that actor and the ID of the User don't change. Those are fixed values. This means that this actor is always uniquely identifiable either by the path, or by the ID. This makes the User an Entity.

Often, a good practice when building actors to represent entities is to use the entity ID as the name of the actor. In general, you should try to model your actor hierarchy to replicate the structure of the entities in the domain as closely as possible.

Domain Value Objects

Value Objects, on the other hand, are different from Entities. A Value Object has no identity beyond the attributes that it contains. Two Value Objects that contain the same data are considered to be the equal; you don't bother trying to distinguish between them. Value Objects, unlike Entities, are immutable. They must be immutable because if their properties change, they become different Value Objects—they are no longer equal.

In Akka, the messages passed between actors are natural Value Objects. Those messages are immutable if we are following best practices and are usually not identifiable. They are just data containers. They might contain references to other Entities, but the message itself is not usually an Entity. We can also use Value Objects as the containers that hold the state of our actors. We can swap in different states as required, but the state itself doesn't have any identity. It is only when it is present inside of the actor that it becomes identifiable. If we were to create two unique actors that both had the same state, the actors would be considered Entities, whereas the state would be considered Value Objects.

Our User actor might have a series of messages that need to be passed to that actor in order to alter its state. For example, if you need to change the name of the user, you might do that by using a message like `SetName`:

```
object User {
    case class SetName(firstName: String, lastName: String)
}
```

In this case, the `SetName` message is a Value Object. If you have two `SetName` objects for which the value of `firstName` and `lastName` is the same, those two messages can be considered equivalent. Whether you send one or the other doesn't matter, the effect on the user is the same. Conversely, if you were to change the value of `first Name` in one of the messages, it would be a different message. Sending it to the user would have a completely different effect. There is no unique identifier for the `SetName` message. There is no way to distinguish one message from the other except by the contents of the message itself. This is what makes it a Value Object.

The messages that you use to pass between actors are called the *message protocol*. A good practice is to embed messages for a particular type of actor in a common protocol object. This can be either in the companion object for the individual actor or it can be a separate protocol object (e.g., `UserProtocol`). The latter case is particularly useful if you want multiple types of actors to handle the same set of messages.

Aggregates and Aggregate Roots

Aggregates are collections of objects within an application. An aggregate creates a logical grouping of many different elements of a system. Every aggregate is bound to an *aggregate root*. An aggregate root is a special entity within the aggregate that has been given responsibility for the other members of that aggregate. One of the properties of an aggregate is that other aggregates are forbidden from holding a reference to anything inside the aggregate. If you want to gain access to some element inside the aggregate, you must go through the aggregate root; you do not access the inner element directly. For instance, if your person aggregate root has an address entity, you don't directly access the address, but instead access the appropriate person, and then reference the contained address.

Aggregates, and their associated roots, are a tricky concept. It can be difficult to determine what is an aggregate in your system, or more importantly, what is the right aggregate root. Generally aggregate roots are the top-level pieces of a system. All of your interactions with the system will in one way or another interface with an aggregate root (with a few exceptions). So how do you determine what your aggregate roots are?

One simple rule is to consider deletion. If you pick a specific Entity in the system and delete it, does that delete other Entities in the system? If your system consists of people who have addresses, and you delete an address, does it delete other parts of the system? In this case, probably not. On the other hand, if you delete a person from the system, there is a good chance that you don't need to keep that person's address around anymore, so in this case, a person might aggregate an address. Keep in mind, however, that although people are often aggregate roots in a system, it is not always the case. Take a bowling score-keeping system as an example. In this system, you might have the concept of a game and a player. The player might seem like a natural candidate for an aggregate root. They have scores, and if you delete a player the scores associated with that player are deleted, too. But if you step up another layer, what happens if you delete a game? Well, you could argue that deleting the game does not delete the player, but that isn't quite accurate. Deleting the game does not delete the person, but if a person is not involved in any games, is that person actually still considered a player? In this case, it might make more sense to say that the game is the aggregate root.

Remember, though, that you might get it wrong. The point isn't to pick the right aggregate root directly from the start. The important thing is to keep the cost of changing your mind later as low as possible.

In Akka, aggregate roots are often represented by parent actors. When you delete/stop those parents, all of their children go with them. But they don't need to be top-level actors. Sometimes, it is beneficial to have a layer or two between the top level and the actual aggregate roots. For example, if your users are the aggregate roots, you might want a layer above the user that will be the parent of all users. In this case, your user is still the aggregate root, but you have another component in your system that is responsible for managing those users. This is especially true when you begin introducing concepts like cluster sharding (see Chapter 2).

Let's look at a very quick example. In a scheduling system, we probably have people that need to be scheduled. We will represent a person using a `Person` actor. But that `Person` might also have a `Schedule`. It might be desirable (especially when using the Actor Model) to represent that `Schedule` by using an actor, as well, as demonstrated here:

```
object Schedule {
  def props = Props(new Schedule)
}

class Schedule extends Actor {
  ...
}

class Person(id: UUID) extends Actor {
  private val schedule = createSchedule()

  protected def createSchedule() = context.actorOf(Schedule.props)
}
```

You can see in this example that the `Person` actor definitely aggregates the `Schedule`. You can't access the `Schedule` without going through the `Person`, and if you delete the `Person` the `Schedule` goes with it. This makes `Person` a candidate for an aggregate. Of course, you can't stop there. You would need to look at the whole picture. Is `Person` a child of some other actor? Does that mean that the other actor is actually the aggregate? These are the types of questions that you need to ask when trying to find your aggregate root.

Repositories

Repositories are where we begin to abstract away our infrastructure concerns. They are used to create an abstraction layer over the top of our storage concerns. The basic approach when working with aggregates in DDD is to go to a repository, retrieve an aggregate from that repository, perform some operation, and then save the aggregate again. This sounds a lot like a database. In fact a repository can be an abstraction over a database, but you need to be careful to not limit yourself to that thinking. Although a repository could be accessing a database, it could also be pulling data from memory, or from disk, or from the web. It might in fact do all of these things. There is nothing that says that a single repository can't have a dependency on multiple storage mechanisms or be transient or computed.

The key to using repositories is to understand that they are abstraction layers. For this reason, they are often represented as a *trait* in Scala. That trait defines how you interface with the repository but hides any implementation details about whether it talks to a database or some other storage mechanism. You then create infrastructure-specific implementations of that trait to be used by the domain code.

In Akka, when using the Actor Model, repositories can be a little tricky. The general flow of a repository involves something resembling an Akka ask. You ask the repository for an instance of some aggregate, you perform an operation on that aggregate, and then you instruct the repository to commit that change. The problem is this violates the principles of "Tell, Don't Ask" (more on that later). Often in Akka, our repositories take on a slightly different appearance. Instead of asking the repository for an instance of a particular aggregate, we instruct the repository to give a message to that aggregate. The repository acts like a "manager." It is the parent of a certain set of actors. We inform that manager that we want a specific actor to process a message. It is then the responsibility of the repository to locate that actor and pass the message on.

We need to remember as well that the purpose of a repository is to abstract away from infrastructure concerns. Our goal when using a repository is usually to reconstitute an aggregate from a database or other storage mechanism. If we are using actors to represent our aggregates this will probably mean loading some data from a database, creating the appropriate actor using that data, and then passing a message to the aggregate. The aggregate itself can still be part of the domain. The interface to the repository is also part of the domain. However, the precise details of the repository implementation are part of the infrastructure, not part of the domain.

Why does this matter? Why is it important to treat the implementation as part of the infrastructure? Our goal is to create a system in which the domain is disconnected from the infrastructure. We don't want to care about whether we are using a SQL database, a NoSQL database, a data file, or any other structure. Ideally, we want to be able to swap in different implementations of the repository if need be. This can be valuable for testing purposes, but it is also valuable for production code as the application evolves. We don't want to assume that our current database implementation is static and will remain so. Instead, we want to assume that it will evolve and prepare for that. As our needs evolve we can write new repository implementations and make use of them without having to rewrite the logic that talks to that repository.

In our scheduling domain, assuming that we have decided that our `Person` is an aggregate, we might have a `PersonRepository` to manage instances of that aggregate. If you are using the Actor Model, that `PersonRepository` should be an actor, as well. In this case, you will want to define an interface to that repository inside of your domain. Because actors communicate through messages rather than through methods, it doesn't make sense to use a trait here. Instead, we define the interface as a message protocol in the domain:

```
object PersonRepository {
  case class Send(userId: UUID, message: Any)
}
```

You can then define a `PersonRepository` in your infrastructure that makes use of that protocol, but how that protocol is used it left to the infrastructure. Here's how you might implement this:

```
class CassandraPersonRepository extends Actor {
  ...
}
```

Because Akka communicates by using `ActorRefs` rather than actor instances, you can pass around a reference to this repository where you need to. Clients using that reference don't need to know they are talking to a `CassandraPersonRepository` rather than a `SQLPersonRepository`. They need only know that the repository makes use of the `PersonRepository` protocol. You can then "Send" a message to the repository, identifying the user to which that message is directed. It is up to the `PersonRepository` to find the appropriate user (or create it) and then deliver the message.

Factories and Object Creation

Factories exist to abstract away the complexities of new domain object creation. Sometimes, the creation of a new domain object is complicated. It may involve wiring multiple pieces together, or pulling some data from data storage. There can be any number of complex operations that need to be performed. Factories differ from repositories only slightly. A factory is intended to abstract away new object creation, whereas a repository is intended to abstract away existing object re-creation. However, often that subtle difference is not enough to warrant the creation of a new abstraction layer. For this reason factories and repositories are sometimes combined, providing methods that will create a new object or return an existing one if possible.

In Akka, a factory operates much the same as a repository. Like with a repository, instead of following an ask pattern, it is often better to use a tell pattern wherein you instruct the factory to create your object and then pass a message to the newly created instance. Again, because of its similarity to a repository, distinguishing between the two is often not really necessary.

Domain Services

When using DDD, the goal is always to try to put your logic into an existing domain object. Usually this means adding to an aggregate root. But sometimes this is difficult. For example, you might have an operation that does not naturally fit into any particular aggregate root, or conversely, you might have an operation that works over multiple aggregate roots. In these cases, it might be difficult to find a suitable domain object to fill the role required. For these situations, we can introduce something called a *service*. A service is a domain object that is there to handle actions that do not naturally fit as an aggregate, but services can interact with aggregates as required.

Generally, we try to leave services as a last resort. If an aggregate fits the role, you should use it. If no existing aggregate fits, you should ask yourself if there is an aggregate that you are missing. Only when you have exhausted other possibilities should you introduce a service instead.

In Akka, services can take many forms. They could be long-lived actors that operate against other aggregate actors. Or, they could be temporary actors that are created to perform some task and then terminated when the task is completed.

An example of a service in the scheduling domain example would be a worker actor that you create to fulfill a particular task. For example, you might want a temporary worker actor to handle a single request:

```
class ScheduleRequestService(request: ScheduleRequest) extends Actor {
  ...
}
```

The job of the `ScheduleRequestService` is to manage any state involved with that particular request and to communicate with whatever aggregates are needed during the fulfillment of the request. After the request has been processed completely, the `ScheduleRequestService` can be terminated. An alternative implementation for this would be to create the `ScheduleRequestService` as a long-lived actor. Instead of taking the request as a constructor parameter, it would instead receive the request as a message. However, to manage all the state for the request, you might still need to create a temporary actor (e.g., `ScheduleRequestWorker`).

Bounded Contexts

The real key to DDD lies not in the small pieces that we use to build our domain. It isn't the aggregates or the repositories that make the real magic happen. What makes DDD special comes in the form of *bounded contexts*. Any system of significant size is going to naturally break down into smaller components. These components can have their own domain. Although that domain can share some elements with the overall system, how those elements are represented might be different depending on the context in which they are used. Trying to build a single, cohesive domain that fits all use cases breaks down quickly. Bounded contexts seek to avoid this problem by recognizing that each context that you operate in might have a different Domain Model.

Take the scheduling example we've been building. When attempting to schedule people on a particular job, we have a domain representation of those people. On the other hand, we have a separate piece of the system that is going to be responsible for maintaining those people and any information about them. Both pieces of the system are dealing with the same people, but they each have very different needs. Whereas the people management side might care about things like addresses and phone numbers, the scheduling system might not. If we were to try to build a Domain Model that suited both purposes, we could hopelessly clutter our code. For that matter, there are aspects of the scheduling side that are completely unrelated to managing the people. When scheduling, it might be necessary to schedule resources that aren't people at all. Those resources might be pieces of hardware, machinery, or vehicles. Trying to shoehorn those into the same structure as we do people is certain to fail.

In addition to a system for managing people, other bounded contexts might exist in the system. We might want a separate context for managing skills. Although it is possible that can end up being part of our people management, it might be that the skills management is significantly large and complex enough that we might want to keep it separate. We might want to do the same with our project management. Again the details of a project might not be necessary for the actual scheduling. When creating a project, we might need to include information like the primary contact for the project. This information is important, but not for the scheduling engine. Again, separating project management from project scheduling can be valuable.

In Akka, a bounded context can take different forms. It might be desirable to create a series of top-level actors in the system, one for each bounded context. Often, however, bounded contexts represent services that are disconnected from one another. They might be separate actor systems tied together by using Akka HTTP. Or, they might be actors tied together by using Akka Remoting or Akka Cluster. They might reside in the same Java Virtual Machine (JVM), but they can also live in separate JVMs, separate machines, or even separate datacenters. In fact, when dividing up your application into bounded contexts, you might discover that although some contexts map naturally to the Actor Model, others might be more suitably implemented by using a more functional architecture or a more traditional object-oriented architecture. The key is that recognizing that each bounded context is separate and distinct allows you to make those decisions as required. You aren't tied to any particular approach. You can experiment with what best fits the bounded context.

This approach to bounded contexts fits very well with modern microservices architectures. In this case, each microservice often represents a single bounded context. More importantly, by separating the application into its constituent parts, you can begin to make decisions about how to distribute and scale it.

In breaking an application into separate bounded contexts and distributing those contexts across multiple machines, you give rise to the idea of distributed domain-driven design (DDDD). Using tools like Akka clustering, cluster sharding, and Akka HTTP, you can take a large system, break it up into separate bounded contexts and then distribute those in ways that would be difficult without the tools Akka provides. Here, the concept of *location transparency* that the Actor Model provides gives you the freedom to distribute actors in myriad different patterns. Whether it is distributing your bounded contexts as Akka HTTP endpoints or distributing actors in a single bounded context using cluster sharding, you are not limited in how you deploy your system. The actual deployment of your actors becomes an implementation detail rather than being an intrinsic part of the application. This opens up the possibility of independently scaling different portions of the system.

Conclusion

Overall, DDD can provide a means to provide the structure a system needs. Applications built without such a structure tend to be much more difficult to understand and maintain, and as a result they lack overall quality. This is especially true with Akka systems built with the Actor Model, because the desirable high level of isolation can make it difficult to see the overall design without DDD.

Now that we have introduced you to both Akka and the Actor Model (and shown you how this merges with the power design approach of DDD), you have the tools necessary to build powerful, scalable, and highly maintainable systems, keeping your system well structured with these established patterns.

In Chapter 4, we will discuss the attributes of good design with actors, and how to best organize your system for concurrent and effective data flow, while safely maintaining the scalability you want.

Good Actor Design

Understanding how to build good actor systems begins at the small scale. The large-scale structures that we build are often the source of our greatest successes or failures in any software project, regardless of whether it uses Akka. But if we don't first understand the smaller building blocks that go into those larger structures, we run the risk of small mistakes propagating throughout the system in a way that makes the code unmaintainable. This problem isn't unique to Akka. If you try to write code using a functional language without first understanding the basics of functional programming, you will run into similar problems.

In this chapter, we talk about how to avoid such issues and apply good principles and practices to building your actors and your system.

Starting Small

As just mentioned, understanding how to build good actor systems must begin at the small scale. We can talk about how to build and connect large-scale actor constructs together, but if we lack a good design at the small scale, we can still easily end up with bottlenecks, blocking operations, and spaghetti code that can cause the application to fail.

The most common mistakes people make when working with Akka happen in the small scale rather than the large end of the spectrum. Even though these problems tend to be smaller in scope than architectural problems, when compounded together they can become significant. Whether it is accidentally exposing mutable state, or closing over that mutable state in a future, it is easy to make mistakes that can render your actor system incomprehensible. You need to remember that although actors address some of the issues you encounter when building concurrent systems, they work only when you use them correctly. If you use them incorrectly, they can create just as many concurrency bugs as any other system. And even though actors can help to address some problems when building concurrent systems, they don't solve every problem. So just as with any concurrent system, you need to watch out for bottlenecks, race conditions, and other problems that might come up.

Think about our sample project management system. In that application, we have separated out bounded contexts like the scheduling service, the people management service, and the project management service. But when we deploy the system we discover something unexpected. The user management service, which was supposed to be a very simple data management service, is not living up to expectations. We are losing data unexpectedly. Digging deeper, we can see that the system was built using a mix of different concurrency paradigms. There are actors and futures mixed together without consideration for what that means. As a result, there are race conditions. We are closing over mutable state inside of multiple threads. We have a series of concurrency problems that could have been avoided.

In the meantime, looking deeper it's evident that our scheduling service isn't handling the load. We expected to have to scale it, due to the fairly complex logic it involves, but now it appears that it is running so poorly that it is jeopardizing the project. We can mitigate the problem by scaling, but even then it might prove to be too slow. Investigating further, it's clear that the application is only capable of handling a small number of concurrent projects. It turns out we have introduced blocking operations that are consuming all the threads, and this in turn is crippling the application.

There are patterns and principles in Akka that you can use to help prevent problems like these. The key is knowing when and where to apply those patterns. When used incorrectly, the patterns can create just as many problems as they solve. But if you apply them correctly, they will give you a strong foundation upon which to build the rest of your system.

Encapsulating State in Actors

One of the key features of actors is their ability to manage state in a thread-safe manner. This is an important feature to understand, but you also need to be aware that there is more than one way to manage that state, and each option might have its uses, depending on the situation. It is also valuable to know those patterns so that if you look into someone else's code you can recognize the pattern and understand the motivation behind it.

Encapsulating State by Using Fields

Perhaps the simplest option for managing state is including the state in mutable private *fields* inside the actor. This is relatively straightforward to implement. It will be familiar to you if you are used to a accustomed imperative style of programming. It is also one of the more common ways mutable state is represented when looking at examples people provide in books, courses, or online.

In our project scheduling domain, we have the concept of a person. A person consists of many different data fields that might be altered. This includes data like first name, last name, business roles, and so on. You can update these fields individually or as a group. A basic implementation of this might look like the following:

```
object Person {
  case class SetFirstName(name: String)
  case class SetLastName(name: String)
  case class AddRole(role: Role)
}

class Person extends Actor {
  import Person._
  private var firstName: Option[String] = None
  private var lastName: Option[String] = None
  private var roles: Set[Role] = Set.empty

  override def receive:Receive = {
    case SetFirstName(name) => firstName = Some(name)
    case SetLastName(name) => lastName = Some(name)
    case AddRole(role) => roles = roles + role
  }
}
```

The basic format will be familiar to those accustomed to object-oriented programming and writing getters and setters in languages like Java. If you're more functional-minded, the presence of mutable state might make you cringe a little, but within the context of an actor, mutable state is safe because it is protected by the Actor Model. If you dig into the standard Scala libraries, you will find that mutable state is actually quite common in what are otherwise pure functions. The mutable state in that case is isolated to within the function and is therefore not shared among different threads. Here, we have isolated the mutable state to within an actor, and due to the single-threaded illusion, that state is protected from concurrent access.

This approach is a good one to use when you are trying to model something simple. If only a few mutable fields or values are involved and the logic that mutates those fields is minimal, it might be a good candidate for this type of approach.

The problem with this approach is that as the complexity increases, it begins to become unmanageable. In our example of an actor representing a person, what happens when it expands and you need to keep state for various pieces of additional information like the address, phone number, and so on? You are adding more fields to the actor, all of which are mutable. They are still safe, but over time as this grows, it could begin to look ugly. Consider as well what happens if the logic around those things is nontrivial—for example, if you begin having to include validation logic for when you set a person's address. Your actor is becoming bloated. The more you add, the worse it will become, as illustrated here:

```scala
class Person extends Actor {
  private var firstName: Option[String] = None
  private var lastName: Option[String] = None
  private var address: Option[String] = None
  private var phoneNumber: Option[String] = None
  private var roles: Set[Role] = Set.empty

  override def receive:Receive = {
    case SetFirstName(name) =>
      firstName = Some(name)
    case SetLastName(name) =>
      lastName = Some(name)
    case SetAddress(address) =>
      validateAddress(address)
      address = Some(address)
    case SetPhoneNumber(phoneNumber) =>
      validatePhoneNumber(phoneNumber)
      phoneNumber = Some(phoneNumber)
    case AddRole(role) => roles = roles + role
  }
}
```

Another issue with this is that actors are inherently more difficult to test than other constructs in Scala because they are concurrent, and this concurrency introduces complexity into your tests. As the complexity of the code increases, so too does the complexity of the tests. Soon, you might find yourself in a situation in which your test code is becoming difficult to understand and tough to maintain, and that poses a problem.

One way to solve this problem is to break the logic out of the actor itself. You can create traits that can be stacked onto the actor. These traits can contain all the logic to mutate the values as appropriate. The actor then becomes little more than a concurrency mechanism. All of the logic has been extracted to helper traits that can be written and tested as pure functions. Within the actor, you then need worry only about the mutability and concurrency aspects. Take a look:

```scala
trait PhoneNumberValidation {
  def validatePhoneNumber(phoneNumber: Option[String]) = {
    ...
  }
}

trait AddressValidation {
  def validateAddress(address: Option[String]) = {
    ...
  }
}
```

```
class Person extends Actor with PhoneNumberValidation with AddressValidation {
  ...
}
```

This technique makes it possible for you to simplify the actor. It also reduces the number of things you need to test concurrently. However, it does nothing to reduce the number of fields that are being mutated or the tests that need to happen around the mutation of those fields. Still, it is a valuable tool to have in your toolbox to keep your actors from growing too large and unmanageable.

So how can you reduce some of that mutable state? How can you take an actor that has many mutable parts and reduce it to a smaller number? There are a few options. One is to reevaluate the structure. Maybe you didn't actually want a single actor for all of the fields. In some cases, it might be beneficial to separate this into multiple actors, each managing a single field or group of fields. Whether you should do this depends largely on the domain. This is less of a technical question and more of a domain-driven design (DDD) question. You need to look at the domain and determine whether the fields in question are typically mutated as a group or as a single field. Are they logically part of a single entity in the domain or do they exist as separate entities? This will help to decide whether to separate additional actors.

But what if you determine that they are logically part of the same entity and therefore the same actor? Is it possible to reduce some of this mutable state within a single actor?

Encapsulating State by Using "State" Containers

In the previous example, you can extract some of the logic from Account into a separate, nonactor-based `PersonalInformation` class. You could extract this into a class or set of classes that are much more type safe, easier to test, and a good deal more functional. This leaves you with just a single `var` to store the entire state rather than having multiple ones, as shown here:

```
object Person {
  case class PersonalInformation(
    firstName: Option[FirstName] = None,
    lastName: Option[LastName] = None,
    address: Option[Address] = None,
    phoneNumber: Option[PhoneNumber] = None,
    roles: Set[Role] = Set.empty
  )
}

class Person extends Actor {
  private var personalInformation = PersonalInformation()

  override def receive: Receive = ...
}
```

This is an improvement. You now have a `PersonalInformation` class that is much easier to test. You can put any validation logic that you want into that state object and call methods on it as necessary. You can write the logic in an immutable fashion, and you can test the logic as pure functions. In fact, if later you decide that you don't want to use an actor, you could eliminate the actor altogether without having to change much (or anything) about `PersonalInformation`. You could even choose not to declare `PersonalInformation` within the companion object for the actor. You could opt instead to move that logic to another location in the same package or move it to a different package or module.

This is a nice technique to use when the logic of your model becomes complicated. It provides the means for you to extract your domain logic completely so that it is encapsulated in the `PersonalInformation` object and your actor becomes pure infrastructure. This reduces everything to a single `var` that is still protected by the single-threaded illusion. But what if you want to eliminate that `var` completely? Can you do that?

Encapsulating State by Using become

Another approach to maintaining this state is by using the `become` feature to store that state. This particular technique also falls more in line with the idea discussed earlier that behavior and state changes are in fact one and the same thing. Using this technique, you can eliminate the `var` completely without sacrificing much in the way of performance. Let's take a look at the code:

```scala
object Person {
  case class PersonalInformation(
    firstName: Option[FirstName] = None,
    lastName: Option[LastName] = None,
    address: Option[Address] = None,
    phoneNumber: Option[PhoneNumber] = None,
    roles: Set[Role] = Set.empty
  )
}

class Person extends Actor {

  override def receive: Receive = updated(PersonalInformation())

  private def updated(personalInformation: PersonalInformation):Receive = {
    case SetFirstName(firstName: FirstName) =>
      context.become(updated(personalInformation
        .copy(firstName = Some(firstName))))
    ...
  }
}
```

This completely eliminates any need for a `var`. Now, rather than altering the state by manipulating that `var`, you are instead altering it by changing the behavior. This changes the behavior so that the next message will have a different `PersonalInforma tion` than the previous one. This is nice because it has a slightly more "functional" feel to it (no more `var`s), but it also maps better to our understanding of the Actor Model. Remember, in the Actor Model, state and behavior are the same thing. Here, we can see how that is reflected in code.

Be wary though. Although this technique has its uses and can be quite valuable, particularly when building finite-state machines, the code is more complex and takes more work to understand. It isn't as straightforward as manipulating a `var`. It might be more complex to follow what is happening in this code if you need to debug it, especially if there are other behavior transitions involved.

So, when should you use this approach rather than using a `var`? This technique is best saved for cases for which you have multiple behaviors, and more specifically, when those behaviors can contain different state objects. Let's modify the example slightly. In the example, most of the values are set as `Options`. This is because when you create your `Person`, those values might not yet be initialized, but they might be initialized later. So, you need a way to capture that fact. But what if, on analyzing the domain, you realize that a person was always created with all of that information present? How could you take advantage of your actor to capture that fact? Here's one way:

```scala
object Person {
  case class PersonalInformation(firstName: FirstName,
                                 lastName: LastName,
                                 address: Address,
                                 phoneNumber: PhoneNumber,
                                 roles: Set[Role] = Set.empty
                                )

  case class Create(personalInformation: PersonalInformation)
}

class Person extends Actor {

  override def receive: Receive = {
    case Create(personalInformation) =>
      context.become(created(personalInformation))
  }

  private def created(personalInformation: PersonalInformation): Receive = {
    ...
  }
}
```

In this example, there are two new states. There is an *initial* state, and a *created* state. In the *initial* state, the personal information has not been provided. The actor therefore accepts only one command (`Create`). After you transition to the *created* state, you can go back to handling the other messages, which allows you to set individual fields. This eliminates the need for optional values because your actor can exist in only one of two states: it is either unpopulated or fully populated. In this case, the state object is valid only in specific states; in this example, it's the "created" state. You could use a `var` and set it as an option to capture this fact, but then you would need to constantly check for the value of that option to ensure that it is what you expect. By capturing the state by using `become` you ensure that you handle only message types that are valid in the current state. This also ensures that the state is always what you expect without requiring additional checks.

When there are other multiple behavior transitions for which each transition might have different state, it is often better to capture that state by using `become` because in this case it simplifies the logic rather than making it more complex. It reduces the cognitive overhead.

Using combinations of `become`, mutable fields, and functional state objects, you can provide rich actors that accurately capture the application's domain. Immutable state objects make it possible for you to create rich domain constructs that can be fully tested independently of your actors. You can use `become` to ensure that your actors can exist only in a set of valid states. You don't need to deal with creating default values for things that are of no concern. And when the actors are simple enough, you can code them by using more familiar constructs like mutable fields with immutable collections.

Mixing Futures with Actors

Futures are an effective way to introduce concurrency into a system. But when you combine them with Akka, you need to be careful. Futures provide one model of concurrency, whereas Akka provides a different model. Each model has certain design principles that it adheres to, and those principles don't always work well together. You should always try to avoid mixing concurrency models within a single context, but sometimes you might find yourself in a situation in which it is required. For those times, you need to be careful to follow the design patterns that allow you to use futures with actors safely.

The heart of the problem is that you are combining two very different models of concurrency. Futures treat concurrency quite differently from actors. They don't respect the single-threaded illusion that actors provide. It therefore becomes easy to break that illusion when using futures with actors. Let's look at some very simple ways by which we can break the single-threaded illusion, beginning with this example:

```
trait AvailabilityCalendarRepository {
  def find(resourceId: Resource): Future[AvailabilityCalendar]
}
```

This is a very simple use of a future. In this case, we have chosen a future to account for the fact that the repository can access a database, and that might take time and can fail. This is an appropriate use of a future and by itself it doesn't create any issues.

The problem in this case arises when you try to use the repository in the context of an actor. Suppose that in order to bring the usage of this repository into your actor system, you decide to create an `Actor` wrapper around it. Our initial naive implementation might look like the following:

```
object AvailabilityCalendarWrapper {
  case class Find(resourceId: Resource)
}

class AvailabilityCalendarWrapper(calendarRepository:
    AvailabilityCalendarRepository) extends Actor {
  import AvailabilityCalendarWrapper._

  override def receive: Receive = {
    case Find(resourceId) =>
      calendarRepository
        .find(resourceId)
        .foreach(result => sender() ! result)
        // WRONG! The sender may have changed!
  }
}
```

This seems fairly simple. The code receives a `Find` message, extracts the `ResourceId`, and makes a call to the repository. That result is then returned to the sender. The problem here is that it breaks the single-threaded illusion. The `foreach` in this code is operating on a future. This means that when you run this code, you are potentially working within a different thread. This could mean that the actor has moved on and is processing another message by the time that `foreach` runs. And that means the sender might have changed. It might not be the actor that you were expecting.

There are multiple ways by which you can fix this problem. You could create a temporary value to hold the correct sender reference, such as in the following:

```
case Find(resourceId) =>
  val replyTo = sender()
  calendarRepository
    .find(resourceId)
    .foreach(result => replyTo ! result)
```

This theoretically fixes the issue. `ReplyTo` will be set to the value of `sender()` at the point at which you are interested in it and it won't change after that. But this isn't ideal for a number of reasons. What if you weren't just accessing the sender? What if there were other mutable states that you need to manipulate? How would you deal with that? But there is a yet more fundamental problem with the preceding code. Without looking at the signature of the repository, how can you verify that you are working with a future? That `foreach` could just as easily be operating on an `Option` or a collection. And although you can switch to using a `for` comprehension or change to using the `onComplete` callback, it still doesn't really highlight the fact that this operation has become multithreaded.

A better solution is to use the Pipe pattern in Akka. With the Pipe pattern you can take a future and "pipe" the result of that future to another actor. The result is that the actor will receive the result of that future at some point or a `Status.Failure` if the future fails to complete. If you alter the previous code to use the Pipe pattern, it could look like the following:

```
import akka.pattern.pipe

object AvailabilityCalendarWrapper {
  case class Find(resourceId: Resource)
}

class AvailabilityCalendarWrapper(calendarRepository:
    AvailabilityCalendarRepository) extends Actor {
  import AvailabilityCalendarWrapper._

  override def receive: Receive = {
    case Find(resourceId) => calendarRepository.find(resourceId).pipeTo(sender())
  }
}
```

There are multiple advantages to using the Pipe pattern. First, this pattern allows you to maintain the single-threaded illusion. Because the result of the future is sent back to the actor as just another message, you know that when you receive it, you won't need any concurrent access to the state of the actor. In this example, the sender is resolved when you call the `pipeTo`, but the message isn't sent until the future completes. This means that the sender will remain correct even though the actor might move on to process other messages.

The other benefit of this pattern is that it is explicit. There is no question when you look at this code as to whether concurrency is happening. It's evident just by looking at the `pipeTo` that this operation will complete in the future rather than immediately. That is the very definition of the Pipe pattern. You don't need to click through to the signature of the repository to know that there is a future involved.

But let's take it a step further. What if you didn't want to immediately send the result to the sender? What if you want to first perform some other operations on it, such as modifying the data so that it adheres to a different format? How does this affect this example? Again, let's look at the naive approach first:

```
import akka.pattern.pipe

object AvailabilityCalendarWrapper {
  case class Find(resourceId: Resource)
  case class ModifiedCalendar(...)
}

class AvailabilityCalendarWrapper(calendarRepository:
    AvailabilityCalendarRepository) extends Actor {
  import AvailabilityCalendarWrapper._

  private def modifyResults(calendar: AvailabilityCalendar):
      ModifiedCalendar = {
    // Perform various modifications on the calendar
    ModifiedCalendar(...)
  }

  override def receive: Receive = {
    case Find(resourceId) =>
      calendarRepository
        .find(resourceId)
        .map(result => modifyResults)
        .pipeTo(sender())
  }
}
```

As before, at first glance this looks OK. The code is still using the Pipe pattern so the sender is safe. But we have introduced a `.map` on the future. Within this `.map` we are calling a function. The problem now is that, again, `.map` is operating within a separate thread. This too creates an opportunity to break the single-threaded illusion. Initially the code might be entirely safe. Later, however, someone might decide to access the sender within the `modifyResults`, or you might decide to access some other mutable state in the calendar. Because it is inside of a function in the `AvailabilityCalendar Wrapper`, you might assume that it is safe to access that mutable state. It is not obvious that this function is actually being called within a future. It is far too easy to accidentally make a change to this code without realizing that you were operating in a separate execution context. So how do you solve that? Here's one way:

```
import akka.pattern.pipe

object AvailabilityCalendarWrapper {
  case class Find(resourceId: Resource)
  case class ModifiedCalendar(...)
}

class AvailabilityCalendarWrapper(calendarRepository:
    AvailabilityCalendarRepository) extends Actor {
  import AvailabilityCalendarWrapper._

  override def receive: Receive = {
```

```
        case Find(resourceId) =>
          calendarRepository.find(resourceId).pipeTo(self)(sender())
        case AvailabilityCalendar(...) =>
          // Perform various modifications on the calendar
          sender() ! ModifiedCalendar(...)
      }
    }
```

This example eliminates the `.map` in this case and brings back the `pipeTo` immediately after the future resolves. This time, though, we pipe back to self and include the sender as a secondary argument in the `pipeTo`. This allows you to maintain the link to the original sender. Again, this is more explicit about what portions of the operation are happening in the future and what portions are happening in the present. There is no longer a possibility of breaking the single-threaded illusion.

Sometimes, you might find yourself in a situation in which the future returns something too generic, like an Integer or a String. In this case, simply using the Pipe pattern by itself can make the code confusing. Your actor is going to need to receive a simple type that is not very descriptive. It would be better if you could enrich the type in some way, perhaps wrapping it in a message. In this case, it is appropriate to use a `.map` on the future for the purpose of converting the message to the appropriate wrapper, as long as you keep that operation as simple and as isolated as possible. For example:

```
ourFuture.map(result => Wrapper(result)).pipeTo(self)
```

The only operation we are making within the `.map` is to construct the wrapper type. Nothing more. This type of `.map` on a future is considered to be low risk enough that you can use it within an actor. The truth is that even this code introduces some risk. Where is `Wrapper` defined? Does it access mutable state somewhere during its construction? It is still possible to make a mistake with this code, but as long as you are following best practices, it will be highly unlikely. For that reason this code is generally considered acceptable.

You need to keep in mind that within an actor there are many things that might be considered mutable state. The "sender" is certainly one form of mutable state. A mutable `var` or a mutable collection is also mutable state. The actor's context object also contains mutable state. `Context.become`, for example, is making use of mutable state. For that matter an immutable `val` that is declared in the parameters of a receive method could be mutable state because the receive method can change. Even access to a database that supports locking still constitutes mutable state. Although it might be "safe," it is in fact mutating some state of the system.

In general, you should favor pure functions within actors wherever possible. These pure functions will never read or write any of the state of the actor, instead relying on the parameters passed in, and returning any modified values from the function. These can then be safely used to modify the mutable state within the actor. Pure functions can also be extracted out of the actor itself, which can ensure that you don't access any mutable state in the actor itself. This makes it possible for you to use those functions in a thread-safe manner within the context of an actor.

When you do find yourself using impure functions within an actor, you need to ensure that you do so within the context of the single-threaded illusion. To do so, you should always prefer the Pipe pattern when working with futures. Sometimes, it can be beneficial to create a wrapper like you did for the repository. This wrapper isolates the future so that you only worry about it in one place and the rest of the system can ignore it. But even better is when you can avoid the future completely and use other techniques in its place.

Ask Pattern and Alternatives

The Ask pattern is a common pattern in Akka. Its usage is very simple and it serves very specific use cases. Let's quickly review how it works.

Suppose that you want to make use of the "wrapper" actor that was introduced earlier. You want to send the "Find" message, and then you need the result of that. To do this using the Ask pattern, you might have something like the following:

```
import akka.pattern.ask
import akka.actor.Timeout
import scala.concurrent.duration._

implicit val timeout = Timeout(5.seconds)
val resultFuture = (availabilityCalendar ?
    AvailabilityCalendarWrapper.find(resourceId)).mapTo[AvailabilityCalendar]
```

In this example, you are using the Ask pattern to obtain a `Future[Any]`. It then uses the `mapTo` function to convert that future into a `Future[AvailabilityCalendar]`.

This is a very helpful pattern when you have an operation for which you need to guarantee success within a certain amount of time. In the event of a failure, you will receive a failed future. In the event that the operation takes too long or doesn't complete, you will also receive a failed future. This can be very useful for situations in which a user is waiting on the other end. The Ask pattern therefore can be quite common when building web apps or REST APIs or other applications that have an agreed-upon time limit.

Problems with Ask

You need to be careful with this approach, though. On its own, there is nothing wrong with it, and in many cases it represents exactly what you want. The problems arise when you begin to overuse this pattern. The Ask pattern has a lot of familiarity. It bears similarity to the way functional programming works. You call a function with some set of parameters, and that function returns a value. That's what we are doing here, but instead of a function, we are talking to an actor. But where the functional model emphasizes a request/response pattern, the Actor Model usually works better with a "Tell, Don't Ask" approach.

Let's explore an example that shows how overusing the Ask pattern can break down. For this example, we will leave our domain behind so that we can focus on just the problem.

Suppose that you have a series of actors. Each actor has the job of performing some small task and then passing the result to the next actor in a pipeline. At the end, you want some original actor to receive the results of the processing. Let's also assume that the entire operation needs to happen within a 5-second window. Let's take a look at the code:

```scala
import akka.pattern.{ask, pipe}

case class ProcessData(data: String)
case class DataProcessed(data: String)

class Stage1() extends Actor {

  val nextStage = context.actorOf(Props(new Stage2()))

  override def receive: Receive = {
    case ProcessData(data) =>
      val processedData = processData(data)
      implicit val timeout = Timeout(5.seconds)
      (nextStage ? ProcessData(processedData)).pipeTo(sender())
  }
}

class Stage2 extends Actor {

  val nextStage = context.actorOf(Props(new Stage3()))

  override def receive: Receive = {
    case ProcessData(data) =>
      val processedData = processData(data)
      implicit val timeout = Timeout(5.seconds)
      (nextStage ? ProcessData(processedData)).pipeTo(sender())
  }
}

class Stage3 extends Actor {

  override def receive: Receive = {
    case ProcessData(data) =>
      val processedData = processData(data)
      sender ! DataProcessed(processedData)
  }
}
```

This code will certainly work and get the job done. But there a few oddities present in the solution. The first issue is the timeouts. Each stage, except for the last, has a 5-second timeout. But here is the problem. The first phase uses 5 seconds. But presumably the second phase will consume some amount of that 5 seconds. Maybe it consumes 1 second. Therefore, when you go to send a message to the next phase, you don't really want a 5-second timeout anymore; you want a 4-second timeout. Because if the third phase takes 4.5 seconds, the second phase would succeed but the entire process would still fail because the first timeout of 5 seconds would be exceeded. The problem here is that the first timeout, the original 5 seconds, is important to the application. It is critical that this operation succeeds within the 5-second window. But all the other timeouts after that are irrelevant. Whether they take 10 seconds or 2 seconds doesn't matter, it's only that single 5-second timeout that has value. Because we have overused the Ask pattern here, we are forced to introduce timeouts at each stage of the process. These arbitrary timeouts create confusion in the code. It would be better if we could modify the solution so that only the first timeout is necessary.

The key here is that every time you introduce a timeout into the system, you need to think about whether that timeout is necessary. Does it have meaning? If the timeout fails, is there some action that can be taken to correct the problem? Do you need to inform someone in the event of a failure? If you answer "yes" to these questions, the Ask pattern might be the right solution. But, if there is already a timeout at another level to handle this case, perhaps you should try to avoid the Ask pattern and instead allow the existing mechanism to handle the failure for you.

Accidental Complexity

There is another problem with the code in the previous example. There is a complexity involved in using the Ask pattern. Behind the scenes, it is creating a temporary actor that is responsible for waiting for the results. This temporary actor is cheap, but not free. We end up with something like that shown in Figure 4-1.

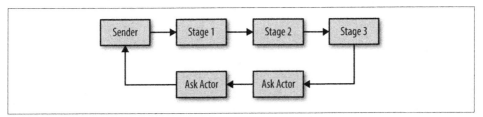

Figure 4-1. Overusing Ask

In the figure, you see the details happening inside the seemingly simple Ask.

We have created a more complex message flow than we really need. We have introduced at least two temporary actors that must be maintained by the system. Granted, that happens behind the scenes without our intervention, but it still consumes resources. And if you look at the diagram and try to reason about it, you can see that there is additional complexity here that you don't really want. In reality, what you would prefer is to bypass the middle actors and send the response directly to the sender. What you really want is to Tell, not Ask.

Alternatives to Ask

There are multiple ways that you could fix this pipeline. One option, given the trivial nature of the example, would be to use the `forward` method. By forwarding the message rather than using the Tell operator, you ensure that the final stage in the pipeline has a reference to the original sender. This eliminates the need for the timeouts and it would eliminate the temporary actors acting as middlemen, as demonstrated here:

```
class Stage1() extends Actor {

  val nextStage = context.actorOf(Props(new Stage2()))

  override def receive: Receive = {
    case ProcessData(data) =>
      val processedData = processData(data)
      nextStage.forward(ProcessData(processedData))
  }
}
```

Another approach to eliminating the Ask would be to pass a `replyTo` actor along as part of the messages. You could include a reference to the actor that is expecting the response. Then, at any stage of the pipeline you would have access to that actor to send it the results or perhaps to back out of the pipeline early if necessary:

```
case class ProcessData(data: String, replyTo: ActorRef)
case class DataProcessed(data: String)

class Stage1() extends Actor {

  val nextStage = context.actorOf(Props(new Stage2()))

  override def receive: Receive = {
    case ProcessData(data, replyTo) =>
      val processedData = processData(data)
      nextStage ! ProcessData(processedData, replyTo)
  }
}

class Stage2 extends Actor {

  val nextStage = context.actorOf(Props(new Stage3()))

  override def receive: Receive = {
    case ProcessData(data, replyTo) =>
      val processedData = processData(data)
```

```
      nextStage ! ProcessData(processedData, replyTo)
  }
}

class Stage3 extends Actor {

  override def receive: Receive = {
    case ProcessData(data, replyTo) =>
      val processedData = processData(data)
      replyTo ! DataProcessed(processedData)
  }
}
```

A final approach would be to pass a Promise as part of the message. Here, you would
send the Promise through the pipeline so that the final stage of the pipe could simply
complete the Promise. The top level of the chain would then have access to the future
that Promise is completing, and you could resolve the future and deal with it appropriately (using pipeTo). The following example shows how to do this:

```
case class ProcessData(data: String, response: Promise[String])

class Stage1() extends Actor {

  val nextStage = context.actorOf(Props(new Stage2()))

  override def receive: Receive = {
    case ProcessData(data, response) =>
      val processedData = processData(data)
      implicit val timeout = Timeout(5.seconds)
      nextStage ! ProcessData(processedData, response)
  }
}

class Stage2 extends Actor {

  val nextStage = context.actorOf(Props(new Stage3()))

  override def receive: Receive = {
    case ProcessData(data, response) =>
      val processedData = processData(data)
      implicit val timeout = Timeout(5.seconds)
      nextStage ! ProcessData(processedData, response)
  }
}

class Stage3 extends Actor {

  override def receive: Receive = {
    case ProcessData(data, response) =>
      val processedData = processData(data)
      response.complete(Success(processedData))
```

```
    }
  }
```

Each of these approaches is valid, and depending on the situation, one might fit better than the other. The point is to realize that you should use Ask only in very specific circumstances. Ask is designed to be used for situations in which either you need to communicate with an actor from outside the system, or you need to use a request/response–style approach and a timeout is desirable. If you find you need to introduce a timeout into a situation that doesn't warrant one, you are probably using the wrong approach.

Commands Versus Events

Messages to and from actors can be broken down into two broad categories: commands and events.

A command is a request for something to happen in the future, which might or might not happen; for instance, an actor might choose to reject or ignore a command if it violates some business rule.

An event is something that records an action that has *already taken place*. It's in the past, and can't be changed—other actors or elements of the system can react to it or not, but they cannot modify it.

It is often helpful to break down the actor's protocol—the set of classes and objects that represents the messages this actor understands and emits—into commands and events so that it is clear what is inbound and what is outbound from this actor. Keep in mind, of course, that an actor *could* consume both commands and events, and emit both as well.

You can often think of an actor's message protocol as its API. You are defining the inputs and outputs to the actor. The inputs are usually defined as commands, whereas the outputs are usually defined as events. Let's look at a quick example:

```
object ProjectScheduler {
  case class ScheduleProject(project: Project)
  case class ProjectScheduled(project: Project)
}
```

Here, we have defined a very simple message protocol for the `ProjectScheduler` actor. `ScheduleProject` is a command. We are instructing the `ProjectScheduler` to perform an operation. That operation is not yet complete and therefore could fail. On the other hand, `ProjectScheduled` is an event. It represents something that happened in the past. It can't fail because it has already happened. `ScheduleProject` is the input to the actor and `ProjectScheduled` is the output. If we weren't using actors and we wanted to represent this functionally, it could look something like this:

```
class ProjectScheduler {
  def execute(command: ScheduleProject): ProjectScheduled = ...
}
```

Understanding the difference between commands and events in a system is important. It can help you to eliminate dependencies. As a small example, consider the following frequently asked question: why is the `ProjectScheduled` part of the `ProjectScheduler`'s message protocol rather than being part of the protocol for the actor that receives it? The simple answer is that it is an event rather than a command. The more complete answer, though, is that it avoids a bidirectional dependency. If we moved it to the message protocol of the actor that receives it, the sender would need to know about the `ProjectScheduler`'s message protocol, and the `ProjectScheduler` would need to know about the sender's message protocol. By keeping the commands and the resulting events in the same message protocol, the `ProjectScheduler` doesn't need to know anything about the sender. This helps to keep your application decoupled.

A common practice, as just illustrated, is to put the message protocol for the actor into its companion object. Sometimes, it is desirable to share a message protocol among multiple actors. In this case, a *protocol* object can be created to contain the messages instead, as shown here:

```
object ProjectSchedulerProtocol {
  case class ScheduleProject(project: Project)
  case class ProjectScheduled(project: Project)
}
```

Constructor Dependency Injection

When you create Props for your actor, you can include an explicit reference to another actor. This is simple to do, and is often a good approach.

Here is an example of direct injection of another `ActorRef` when an actor is created:

```
val peopleActor: ActorRef = ...
val projectsActor: ActorRef = system.actorOf(ProjectsActor.props(peopleActor))
```

However, if your actors have a number of references, or the order of instantiation means that the necessary reference isn't available until after the receiving actor is already constructed, you must look for other means.

actorSelection via Path

One option is to refer to the destination actor via its path, as opposed to its reference. This requires that you know the path, of course, possibly accessing it via a static value in the destination actor's companion object.

A path can be resolved only to an `actorSelection`, however, not an actual actor reference. If you want access to the actor reference, you must send the identify message, and have the reply give us the reference. Or, you simply send your messages to the actor selection directly.

Actor selections have their own problems, though. An actor selection is unverified until you send the `Identify` message. This means that there might or might not be an actor on the other end. This in turn means that when you send a message to a selection, there is no guarantee that there will be an actor on the other end to receive it. In addition, a selection can include wildcards. This means that there might actually be more than one actor on the other end, and when you send a message you are in fact broadcasting it to all actors. This might not be what you want.

Actor selections, when not used carefully, can also lead to increased dependencies. Often, if you are using an actor selection, it implies that you have not carefully thought about your actor hierarchy. You are falling back to an actor selection because you need to reference an actor that is part of a different hierarchy. This creates coupling between different areas of your actor system and makes them more difficult to break apart or distribute later. You can think of this as being similar to littering your code with singleton objects, which is usually considered a bad practice.

Actor reference as a message

A better way to go for more complex dependencies between actors is to send the actor reference as a message to the actor that needs it—for example, you effectively "introduce yourself" to the actor that needs to send a message to you by encapsulating an actor reference in a specific type (so that it can be differentiated by the receive method of the destination actor), and then holding the passed value in the destination actor for later use.

This technique is essentially what we introduced when we used a `replyTo` actor in the message protocol when we were discussing the Ask pattern. The `replyTo` is a way to introduce one actor to another so that the first actor knows where to send messages.

This method demands a little more thought, requiring you to design your hierarchy in such a way that the necessary actors can talk to one another. This additional care is good because it means that you are thinking about the overall structure of the application, rather than just worrying about the individual actors. But you need to be careful here, as well. If you find that you're spending too much effort in passing reference to actors around through messages, it might still mean that you have a poorly defined hierarchy.

Conclusion

In summary, by keeping in mind a few basic principles and techniques, you can create actors that retain cohesion, avoid unnecessary blocking and complexity, and allow the data flow within your actor system to be as smooth and concurrent as possible.

Now that you have seen how individual actors can best be structured, we will raise our level of abstraction to consider the flow of data through the entire system, and how correct actor interactions support that flow.

CHAPTER 5

Good Data Flow

In Chapter 4, you saw some of the ways that you can implement individual actors and some of the pitfalls you can encounter when doing so. Now you need to consider how you can use those actors to build up systems. A single actor alone isn't much help to us. It's only by combining them that we unlock the real potential of Akka. In this chapter, we take a look at some patterns to follow when using multiple actors. We also introduce the concept of Akka Streams, which provides a domain-specific language for streaming messages.

Throughput Versus Latency

Before we go too far discussing how to combine actors effectively, let's digress briefly to talk about throughput versus latency.

When we measure our code to determine its performance characteristics, often we are measuring how long a particular action takes. We measure from the moment that action is initiated, to the moment it completes. It might take 10 milliseconds or perhaps 10 seconds. In either case, we call this latency.

Sometimes, instead of measuring how long a particular action takes, we will instead measure how many actions can occur in a specific amount of time. Here we aren't concerned with how long each individual action takes, just how many of them we can complete within a fixed amount of time. For example, we might measure how many actions we can perform in 10 seconds. In this case, we are measuring throughput.

Whether you measure latency or throughput, you always need to look at the values through the lens of your domain. In some domains, a 10-second latency, or even a 10-hour latency, might be more than sufficient, whereas in other domains it is far too long. You need to consider the domain in which these measurements were taken and whether those measurements represent a good user experience.

But when you build highly concurrent systems, you can't simply look at one measurement or the other. You need both throughput and latency. If you measure only one or the other, you get an incomplete picture that can be quite misleading. Let's consider a couple of examples.

Suppose that a user logs into your system. You measure the latency of this login and it takes 500 milliseconds. From a user perspective, 500 milliseconds isn't that noticeable. If a login takes 500 milliseconds, the user is probably happy and your system is probably working just fine. But that is purely a measure of latency. When you actually turn on the system, you find that you have users waiting as long as 10 seconds to log in! What happened?

Because you measured the latency alone, you failed to account for the fact that the system (for whatever reason) is basically single threaded. Maybe there is a shared resource on which each operation has to block. Maybe you literally allocated only a single thread to do the work. Whatever the case, if each user takes 500 milliseconds and 20 users attempt to log in at the same time, either those users are going to have to wait in line, or they are going to need to fail. So, although the first user was able to log in within 500 milliseconds, the last person in the queue had to wait a full 10 seconds.

What if you measured only throughput, instead? When you do so, you discover that 500 users can log in within 10 seconds. In this case, 500 people logging in within 10 seconds seems reasonable. So you don't need to do any more than that, right? Or do you?

In this scenario, you have measured the throughput but ignored the latency. You discovered that you can have 500 users logged in within 10 seconds, but you didn't bother to see how long each user takes. If it takes the full 10 seconds for each user and you are just doing 500 users at the same time, you might still have created a terrible user experience. If an application consistently takes 10 seconds just to log in the user, there is a good chance the users are going to walk away.

It's only by measuring both throughput and latency that you can truly understand the full picture. You need to understand not just how long events take, but how many events can happen at once. Using this information, you can detect the true bottlenecks in your system and work to resolve them.

Now that you understand the basics of throughput and latency, let's take a look at how you can build actor systems that optimize both.

Streams

When we build software systems, we often talk about building streams of data. These are processes wherein the data goes through some series of steps, one after the other, to produce some output. Generally, when we talk about streams, there is an assumption of order. If you put two pieces of data into the stream, you expect their transformed output to come back in the order in which the inputs were sent. Of course, when you introduce concurrency into the mix that changes. Suddenly, you can send the two inputs in order but the outputs come back reversed. Sometimes, that's OK, but often it isn't. So, how can you use a concurrent system like Akka to build streams in which you can still have a guarantee of order?

Recall that actors in Akka use a mailbox. That mailbox acts like a queue. It operates on a first-in/first-out basis. This means that you can guarantee that whatever we put into a single actor, the outputs will return in the expected order. It is this concept of an ordered mailbox that allows you to build streams using Akka.

You can use ordered mailboxes to pass messages between a discrete set of actors. If you are careful with how you do it, you can take advantage of concurrency and yet still keep the ordering guarantees. Figure 5-1 shows what this might look like.

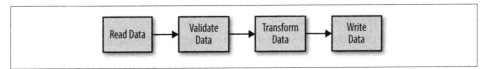

Figure 5-1. Pipeline of actors maintaining message ordering

The figure depicts a very basic stream. Some data is read, and then it is validated, transformed, and written. You could implement this easily without actors. You could implement each step as a blocking operation so that you could guarantee that data being read would be written in the same order. Of course this isn't particularly fair with how you share your resources. If you are waiting for the write to complete, nothing upstream can take place because you are blocked.

If, however, you implement each of these stages as an actor, it opens up some interesting improvements. Because you have no branch points in this stream, you can still guarantee order just as you could without actors. The Read stage cannot process any more messages until it has passed its current message onto the Validate stage. The Validate stage cannot process any more messages until it passes its message to the Transform stage. But because these are actors, the Read, Validate, Transform, and Write stages can all be working on messages concurrently. The Read stage can accept the first message, pass it on to the Validate stage, and immediately start on the next message. It doesn't need to wait for the message to trickle all the way down to the Write stage. If the Write stage takes a long time to complete, it is possible that messages will back up in the queue until those writes complete, but this also means that the Write stage will be able to begin working on the next message as soon as it completes. It also doesn't need to wait for messages to flow down through the stream. That already happened while you were waiting.

This is a perfect example of how measuring just latency can be deceiving. If you were to measure the latency of each message going through the entire stream, it would appear that the time to process each message completely is equal to the sum of the times from each stage, as shown here:

```
Latency = timeToRead + timeToValidate + timeToTransform + timeToWrite
```

When you measure the values for each of the stages, you might end up with something like the following:

timeToRead	timeToValidate	timeToTransform	timeToWrite
2 ms	2 ms	6 ms	10 ms

Now you could use the equation to determine that the latency was 20 milliseconds. You could then infer that the system can deliver new results every 20 milliseconds, giving you a throughput of 50 messages per second. But if you did, you would be wrong. Although this is true for a single-threaded system, it does not apply to a system built using actors. Using actors, you must account for the fact that each stage can be happening in parallel. The throughput of the system is limited by the slowest stage in the stream—in this case, the Write stage. This means that the throughput could end up being 100 messages per second or one message every 10 milliseconds. By measuring only the latency, you would miss this fact.

One of the major benefits to the actor approach is that it introduces concurrency in the system, without sacrificing determinism. You can still guarantee the message order on both sides of the stream.

Streams like this are a powerful tool for optimizing Akka applications. They allow you to take full advantage of the modern multicore systems to which we have access. But by themselves, they are not going to solve all of our scalability problems. Even though you can see that streams like this can improve throughput, you can't scale like this forever. And there is a hidden cost here. Although our total time to process messages might be better using actors than it would have been using the blocking functions, the reality is that at each stage you can still process only a single message at a time. That means the other messages must sit waiting in a queue, and the length of time in that queue is potentially unbounded. So, although streams are an important tool to have, you need other tools to reach high scalability.

Routers

Although streams give us an ability to improve throughput, we can see that this ability to do so is restricted by the number of stages into which we can break our operation and the time it takes at each stage. We also can see that in certain use cases it might be more efficient to use futures because they have the potential to yield higher throughput. But what if you want to achieve the same level of throughput by using actors? Can you do it?

To improve throughput beyond the level that a stream can provide, you need to be able to process multiple streams at the same time. This is where routers come in. As Figure 5-2 demonstrates, a router is simply an actor that can take a message and route it to one of many actors. Routers are important because they offer the means to scale beyond what a stream can provide, at the cost of introducing nondeterminism.

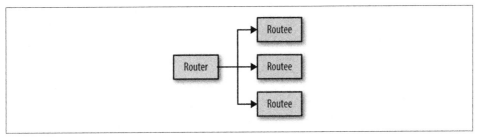

Figure 5-2. A router

Akka provides many different types of routers, but at heart they all serve a similar purpose. A router takes a single message and sends it to one or more routee actors. The logic of which routee to send to or how many of them to send to depends on the implementation of the router. Of course, if the existing routers are insufficient for the needs of your application, you can simply create your own actor that encapsulates the routing logic that you desire.

Because of the branching nature of routers, you lose the determinism that a stream provides. When you send a message through a router, you can't guarantee that the first message in will be the first message out. Depending on the routees it passes through and how the threads have been allocated, it is possible that the messages might leave the system in any order. The trick then is to ensure that you use routers for cases in which the message order is not important, and use streams for cases in which it is important.

Often, when you build systems for which order is important, it is only important at a certain level of the system. For example, in our sample project management domain, when processing requests, it might be critical that certain requests are processed in order. If we are attempting to commit someone to a project, having messages arrive out of order can be disastrous. We can end up committing someone to a project who is actually unavailable. Or we might end up agreeing to a contract that we can't possibly fulfill. It might be important that at certain levels of the application we process messages in a very specific order. On the other hand, there might be areas of the system in which that requirement is less critical. A very simple example is that you might need messages for a particular user to be processed in order, but you might not require that messages be in order across multiple users. In this case, it is possible to design a stream that provides the ordering guarantee when processing an individual user, while using a router in order to process multiple users in parallel, as demonstrated in the setup shown in Figure 5-3.

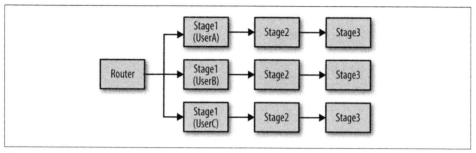

Figure 5-3. Routers and streams

We have created a router that has the job of directing messages to one of three streams. All messages for UserA go to the first stream, all messages for UserB go to the second stream, and all messages for UserC are sent to the third stream. You can create this setup by using a router with consistent hashing logic. You could also do it by using a custom router. This setup is also common when using Akka cluster sharding, which we will discuss later. Because all messages for a particular user will go to the same stream, it's possible to maintain your ordering guarantee within that user. However, across multiple users, for which the ordering doesn't matter, you take advantage of the router to allow scaling. You have introduced nondeterminism into the system, but at a level at which it doesn't violate the system requirements.

With this new structure, you can now process more messages concurrently. Even though each stream is capable of handling only three concurrent messages due to the limit of three stages, you can now process more of those streams at the same time. In Figure 5-3, you can now potentially be processing up to nine messages at the same time (three streams multiplied by three stages). And all of this without sacrificing the ordering guarantees that the application might require.

Another benefit to using routers is that within a single stream there can be stages of that stream in which you need to perform multiple tasks, but the order of those tasks doesn't matter. For example, if you need to check the availability for a person across a longer time period, you might want to check each date individually and aggregate the results. The order in which this happens isn't really relevant. It would be fine to process each day concurrently. Here is an area in which you use something like a router to "branch out" and perform checks. This in turn can improve your end-to-end latency because some of the operations are running concurrently, so the total time to complete is reduced.

Routers are a critical piece of the puzzle. Whether you are using Akka routers or simply implementing your own actors that route messages to other actors, you need them, not only to accommodate scaling out, but also to allow us to scale up. Routers make it possible to use system resources more fully, and more importantly, to reduce bottlenecks that might occur. They are a tool with which we can improve both throughput and latency, and as such they are critical to building highly scalable systems.

Mailboxes

During our discussion about streams and routers, we have been ignoring a glaring issue: the *slow consumer*. A slow consumer occurs when we are able to produce more messages in one part of the system than can be processed in another part. The natural result is that the mailbox for the consumer grows in size over time—in the worst case, the system begins to experience memory issues if we are not using a queuing mechanism that can page out to disk as needed.

A temporary, small surge of message volume from a producer that results in a growing queue for a short period is not necessarily a problem. The problem comes when this is a normal situation, and the queue is growing faster than it is shrinking most of the time, or when the surge is large enough to overrun the available memory.

At its heart, this is a design problem, not a deployment or configuration issue. You can't solve it by tuning, and it probably shouldn't be solved by just having a higher capacity queue between the two parts. There are patterns that can help us here, but before we discuss them, let's first look at the details of the mailboxes and how they might help.

Mailboxes can generally be placed into one of two categories: *bounded mailboxes* and *unbounded mailboxes*. The default is an unbounded mailbox, so we will discuss it first.

Unbounded Mailboxes

Unbounded mailboxes are the default in Akka. When used properly, an unbounded mailbox is sufficient for most use cases. If you use them improperly, however, they can lead to out-of-memory issues. If the actor can't process messages fast enough, you can end up pushing messages into the mailbox until the system runs out of memory.

This out-of-memory error is problematic. When it happens, it isn't just going to kill that actor, it is going to bring down the entire application. Obviously, this is not ideal. Application designers have developed a fear of the unbounded mailbox. Using it is deemed dangerous because of the problems it can cause, and yet it is the default mailbox. How can that be? Why would the default choice for a mailbox be one that could potentially bring down the entire system? Shouldn't we instead choose a mailbox type that prevents this issue?

The reality is that the mailbox isn't the problem. If you take a pail to the sink to fill with water and walk away while the water is running, what is going to happen to the pail? It will fill up and overflow. But is that the fault of the pail? Or is it a problem with a system that has no checks in place to prevent the overflow? Wouldn't it be better if someone or some mechanism were there to shut off the flow in the event that the pail reached its capacity? We will talk about how we can implement systems like this, but first let's consider an alternative mailbox type.

Bounded Mailboxes

Bounded mailboxes seem like the solution to the memory overflow, and in the right use case, they are. However, just as with unbounded mailboxes, you need to be aware of how they work in order to apply them in the proper situation. With a bounded mailbox, you set a limit on how many messages it can hold. When the number of messages exceeds that limit, the mailbox will perform some action to alleviate the problem. What that action is depends on the type of mailbox, which fall into one of two categories: a *blocking bounded mailbox* or a *nonblocking bounded mailbox*.

Blocking bounded mailboxes were present in previous versions of Akka, but they have been been removed. One of the key reasons for their removal is that they were misleading and potentially dangerous. The idea behind a blocking bounded mailbox is that if the mailbox were full, any further inserts to that mailbox would be blocked until the mailbox was cleared. This meant that the thread attempting to do the insert would be blocked and the system would slow down. This in theory would allow the consumer to catch up. There are two problems here. The first is what happens if that actor is remote? There is no communication back and forth between remote actors and local actors about the size of the mailbox. It is therefore impossible to block the sender. The result is that when dealing with remote actors, blocking mailboxes just didn't work. A blocking bounded mailbox became an unbounded mailbox, and the out-of-memory issue returned.

The second problem is a bit more subtle. Suppose that you use a blocking mailbox to block the thread. Let's further assume that you have a limit of four threads and all of our actors are running within that thread pool. Now suppose that four actors attempt to send a message to a slow consumer whose mailbox is full. Those four actors are going to have to block. They will block the threads and they will wait. In the meantime, the slow consumer is supposed to catch up. But the slow consumer is operating in the same thread pool—a thread pool that was limited to four threads, all of which are now blocked. This means that there are no threads left for the consumer to operate on and you have now hit a deadlock.

Speaking more generally, the real problem with a bounded blocking mailbox is that it creates a synchronous dependency between actors. This violates the ideals of the Actor Model, which has actors communicating with one another via asynchronous message passing. Creating a blocking bounded mailbox breaks the model. Therefore, blocking bounded mailboxes have been removed.

So what about nonblocking bounded mailboxes? How do they work? For a nonblocking bounded mailbox to work, you need to know what to do when the mailbox overflows. You can't block and slow down the producer and you can't stash the overflow because that would suggest the mailbox is unbounded. Thus, when the mailbox overflows, you would need to throw away the messages. There aren't really any other feasible options. Of course, this results in message loss, but remember that Akka's delivery guarantee is *at most once*. Throwing away messages fits within this delivery guarantee. If a stronger guarantee is required, you need to be prepared to resend messages by using tools like `AtLeastOnceDelivery`, which we'll discuss in detail later.

Unbounded mailboxes have the flaw that they can overflow their memory. Bounded mailboxes have the flaw that they can lose messages. So what if a situation arises for which the mailbox absolutely cannot overflow and it's unacceptable to lose messages? How do you handle that?

Of course, the best solution to the slow-consumer problem is to make the consumer faster. If it is possible to horizontally scale the consumer—perhaps by having many instances of the consumer—the slow consumer issue doesn't happen at all. When this isn't possible, you must reevaluate the design and the message guarantees; you might be able to adjust the system (by allowing messages to be processed out of order, for instance) to allow the consumer to be scaled.

If you can't avoid the slow consumer altogether, you must seek alternative patterns to solve the problem.

Work Pulling

One solution to slow consumers is to, in essence, "reverse" the normal responsibilities of the participants, having the consuming component *pull* messages, rather than having the producer *push* them.

In this scenario, you have a master actor to manage the messages and a series of worker actors. The master actor doesn't do any real work; instead, it just delegates to the worker actors. The flow of messages in this case works as follows (see Figure 5-4):

1. Master receives new work.
2. Master notifies one or more workers that work is available (`WorkAvailable`).
3. A worker, who is available to process the message, notifies the master that it is ready for more work (`GetWork`).
4. Master sends work item to the available worker.

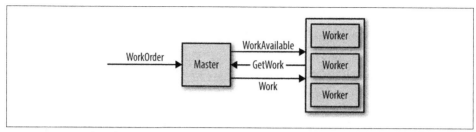

Figure 5-4. Work Pulling pattern

The advantage to this pattern is that it eliminates the possibility of overflow in the worker's mailbox. The worker's mailbox will have only a small number of messages in it at any given time.

The key to implementing this pattern is that the master needs to be capable of slowing down the work flow. This might mean pulling work from a file or database when needed, or it might mean discarding incoming messages. If the master cannot control the work flow in this manner, you might have just moved the problem: rather than the workers overflowing their mailboxes, the master ends up with that problem.

When building a distributed system, the master actor is often implemented as a cluster singleton to ensure that there is only one master at any given time. As long as the master can control the rate of flow, this works well, but if it can't, it becomes a bottleneck, and you might need to look at alternative options.

A big benefit to this pattern is that it is very easy to scale up or down as the load increases or decreases. As new workers come online, they can notify the master of their availability, and the master can begin distributing work to them. This means that if the master begins to back up due to the workers being overloaded, you can simply scale up the number of workers. In a distributed system, this is especially true because the workers can be brought up on new nodes in a cluster, probably running on different hardware.

In our example scheduling domain, if a project is added to the system, that project needs to be scheduled. We could just push a message directly into the system, but scheduling is a time-consuming process. Consequently, if many projects are scheduled simultaneously, we could run into a mailbox problem. To solve this issue, we can use the Work Pulling pattern. When a project is created, we will write a record to a data store. A project scheduler will then pull those records from the database and send a message to a series of worker actors. Each worker actor will then try to schedule that project. Here's how it looks:

```
object ProjectWorker {
  case class ScheduleProject(project: Project)
  case class ProjectScheduled(project: Project)
```

```
    def props(projectMaster: ActorRef): Props =
      Props(new ProjectWorker(projectMaster))
}

class ProjectWorker(projectMaster: ActorRef) extends Actor {
  projectMaster ! ProjectMaster.RegisterWorker(self)

  override def receive: Actor.Receive = {
    case ScheduleProject(project) =>
      scheduleProject(project)
      projectMaster ! ProjectScheduled(project)
  }

  private def scheduleProject(project: Project) = {
    // perform project scheduling tasks
  }
}
```

Here is a simple implementation for our `ProjectWorker` actor. When this actor comes online, it registers itself with the `ProjectMaster` by using the `RegisterWorker` message. If it receives a `ScheduleProject` message, it will perform the necessary scheduling tasks and then send a `ProjectScheduled` message back to `ProjectMaster`. This `ProjectScheduled` message is the cue to the `ProjectMaster` that the worker has completed its task and it is ready to accept more work, as demonstrated here:

```
object ProjectMaster {
  case class ProjectAdded(projectId: ProjectId)
  case class RegisterWorker(worker: ActorRef)
  private case class CheckForWork(worker: ActorRef)

  def props(projectRepository:
      ProjectRepository, pollingInterval: FiniteDuration): Props = {
    Props(new ProjectMaster(projectRepository, pollingInterval))
  }
}

class ProjectMaster(projectRepository:
    ProjectRepository, pollingInterval: FiniteDuration) extends Actor {
  import ProjectMaster._
  import context.dispatcher

  override def receive: Receive = {
    case RegisterWorker(worker) => scheduleNextProject(worker)
    case CheckForWork(worker) => scheduleNextProject(worker)
    case ProjectWorker.ProjectScheduled(project) =>
      scheduleNextProject(sender())
  }

  private def scheduleNextProject(worker: ActorRef) = {
    projectRepository.nextUnscheduledProject() match {
      case Some(project) =>
```

```
        worker ! ProjectWorker.ScheduleProject(project)
      case None =>
        context.system.scheduler.scheduleOnce(pollingInterval, self,
          CheckForWork(worker))
        self ! CheckForWork(worker)
    }
  }
}
```

In this example, the `ProjectMaster` can receive a few different messages; however, the behavior in all cases is the same. If it receives a `RegisterWorker` message, it knows this is a new worker. In that case, it will try to find some work for that new worker to do. If it receives a `ProjectScheduled` message, it knows that a worker has just completed a task. Again, the `ProjectMaster` will try to find more for the worker to do. In the event that it is unable to find more work, it will schedule a `CheckForWork` message to itself to try again later. When the `ProjectMaster` receives this message, it knows that the worker is idle and will again attempt to find more work.

The `ProjectMaster` only pulls work when a worker is idle so there is no risk that the worker's mailbox will overflow. At the same time, the messages for the `ProjectMaster` are triggered only by idle workers. This means that at any given time, there shouldn't be more messages in the `ProjectMaster`'s mailbox than there are workers. So again, there is no risk of mailbox overflow.

A related pattern to work-pulling is to use an external queuing system such as Apache Kafka or RabbitMQ as a means of distributing work to the workers. In this way, you get the safety of a persistent queue or topic, but preserve parallelism. It is possible to write such a queue in Akka directly, but it is frequently more convenient to use an existing tool.

Back Pressure

An alternative to work-pulling is to provide a means for the consumer to provide *back pressure*. Much like the analogy of a pipe with water flowing in it, the data "fills the pipe," and the system exerts pressure back on the sender to slow down the flow, as illustrated in Figure 5-5.

Figure 5-5. Back pressure

This can take the form of a special message that the consumer emits when it is reaching a maximum rate of processing, or it can be supplied by the transport mechanism, as we will see soon.

In either case, the message has the same effect: notify the producer to slow down its rate of production so as not to overwhelm the queue and the consumer.

There are several approaches to back pressure.

Acks

A simple means of producing back pressure is to have the consumer send back to the producer an acknowledgment, usually abbreviated as it is in networking to an "ack." This ack could be identified; for example, it could specify *which* message was received, or it could simply say "OK, I've processed one, you can send one more." Of course, the same technique can be applied for a size greater than one—the consumer, for instance, could confirm processing every hundred or every thousand messages— the principle is the same.

High-Water Marks

Instead of acknowledging messages, singly or in groups, another option is to do the reverse: send a message when the producer should slow down or stop, in response to some value exceeding a so-called high-water mark.

Instead of saying, "I've done X messages, send some more," the high-water mark technique says the reverse: "Things are getting hot, slow down," is the meaning of the message in this case.

You should take care to use a different channel to send the control messages, of course, because a backlog on *that* channel can defeat the operation of the control message, leading to obvious issues.

Queue-Size Monitoring

Tracking the size of the queue between the producer and the consumer is another option; in fact, this can be the high-water mark that is used in the previous technique.

Caution is warranted, however, because it's possible to place additional load on the system by monitoring the queue, given that this is a performance-critical area, especially if the producer and consumer are not singular components—there could be a great many producers and consumers, and they might be separated via a network.

Rate Monitoring

If you have a previously benchmarked consumer, you might be able to find the approximate rate at which messages can be consumed and control the flow entirely from the producer end by using this information.

This technique says, "If the consumer can handle X messages in Y time, the producer must send no more than X messages every Y period." Assuming that all messages take close to the same amount of time to process, this can be a simple technique that requires no direct communication between the producer and consumer.

Like all time-based operations, however, it is subject to variance over time, depending on the load on the overall system, so it is not reliable when conditions change. Suppose that you begin running some new process on the same node as your consumer; suddenly you're not consuming at the same rate as you were before, so the producer will begin sending faster than can be handled.

Of course, it's possible to build a self-tuning system wherein the consumer actually sends a message periodically to the producer, updating its rate information from time to time. This is a bit more complex, but very flexible, and still requires comparatively little communication between the consumer and producer.

The problem with all of these techniques—whether it's work-pulling, back pressure, rate monitoring, or something else—is that they all require extra effort on your part. None of them are built in to the system. When building pure actor-based systems, you need these techniques in order to prevent memory problems, but it would be nice if there were something built in to help you.

Akka Streams

You have seen how streams can improve message throughput and how routers can improve both throughput and latency depending on how they are used. You have also seen how mailboxes can overflow and how you can fix that by using techniques like back pressure. The evolution of these ideas takes the form of Akka *Streams*. Akka Streams are Akka's implementation of Reactive Streams. They take the concepts of streams, routers, back pressure, and more and roll it all into a single consistent domain-specific language (DSL) that allows you to write type-safe streams, including junction points, that support back pressure all the way through. They make it possible to build complex flows of data without having fear of overrunning the actor's mailbox. At the same time, they provide all the same advantages that we got from creating actor streams with routers as branch points.

Akka Streams are built on a few basic concepts. These include sources, sinks, flows, and junctions. Each of these has a role to play when building up a stream of data. We will explore them each in detail so that you can fully understand how they address the problems we face.

To help visualize the role that each of these pieces play, it is helpful to imagine an Akka Stream as a flow of water through a set of pipes. As we explore each concept, we will see how this works.

Source

A source in Akka Streams represents a source of data. This is the origin point of your stream, whether it is a file, a database, or some other input to the system. When back pressure needs to be applied and you need to slow down the system, this is where it will need to occur. There are different ways in which you can slow down the flow depending on what the source of the data is. It might mean slowing down the rate you pull from a file, it might mean buffering data to disk, or it might mean dropping data. It all depends on the nature of the source and what level of control you have over its speed.

Continuing with the plumbing analogy, the source is the origin of the water. Whether it's coming from a river, a lake, or a reservoir, at some point, you need to draw water from that source and pump it through the pipes. Imagine then that there is a giant lake from which you want to draw water. You put a pump in the lake and begin connecting pipes (Figure 5-6). The pump is the source of the water. We can speed up or slow down the rate that water flows through the system by adjusting the flow rate on the pump.

Figure 5-6. Plumbing source

There are many different ways in which you can build a source. A source can be constructed by using a simple iterator like the following:

```
val positiveIntegers = Source.fromIterator(Iterator.from(1))
```

A simple case like this is not always possible. Sometimes, you need something more complicated. There are a variety of different techniques available to implement custom sources using graph stages. Let's look at one here:

```
class RandomIntegers extends GraphStage[SourceShape[Int]] {
  private val out: Outlet[Int] = Outlet("NumbersSource")
  override val shape: SourceShape[Int] = SourceShape(out)

  override def createLogic(inheritedAttributes: Attributes): GraphStageLogic = {
    new GraphStageLogic(shape) {
      setHandler(out, new OutHandler {
```

```
        override def onPull(): Unit = {
          push(out, Random.nextInt())
        }
      })
    }
  }
}
```

A source, `GraphStage`, is going to consist of one outlet. This outlet is the output from the source. It connects to other elements in the stream. If the source is a pump, the outlet is the connector that attaches to the pipes. This outlet is passed to a shape—in this case, a `SourceShape`. There are other shapes that you could use depending on the circumstances. A `SourceShape` is a simple shape that has just one outlet, as illustrated in Figure 5-7, but if necessary you can create shapes with multiple outlets.

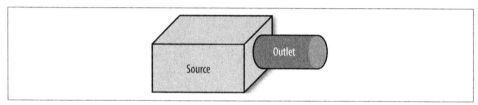

Figure 5-7. Plumbing

From here, you apply `GraphStageLogic`. The `GraphStageLogic` has an `OutHandler` with a corresponding `onPull` method. The `onPull` method will determine what action to take when data is requested from the stream. In this case, you have implemented something very simple (a random number), but this can become as complex as you need it to be. It can read from a file, draw from a buffer, or whatever you need it to do.

One key to implementing this is that any mutable state must be contained within the `GraphStageLogic`. The `GraphStage` is just a template for the logic. It is reusable and can potentially be used in multiple streams. In all likelihood, you don't want to share state across those streams. The `GraphStageLogic`, on the other hand, will be created each time a stream is created. This means that each time you connect a source to a sink, you will get a new instance of the `GraphStageLogic`.

Sink

A sink in Akka Streams represents the endpoint of the stream. At some point all streams need to end. Without an endpoint, streams don't really have a purpose. Whether we are writing to a database, producing a file, or displaying something in a user interface, the goal of the stream is to produce this output. In fact, for a stream to be complete it needs only two pieces: the source and the sink.

Carrying on with our plumbing analogy, you can imagine that the pump, which is drawing water from the lake, is going to push that water into the pipes so that when the user in the house opens the faucet, water will flow into a sink, as depicted in Figure 5-8. This is the end destination for the water—its endpoint. Of course, it's unreasonable to assume that the sink in the house is connected directly to the pump in the lake without anything between them. Plumbing in the real world doesn't work that way.

Figure 5-8. Plumbing sink

As with a source, there are multiple ways to create a sink. There are very simple examples, like the following:

```
val printString = Sink.foreach[Any](println)
```

This creates a sink that will simply call `println` on any items coming into it. You also can use a `fold` method:

```
val sumIntegers = Sink.fold[Int, Int](0) { case (sum, value) => sum + value }
```

The `fold` method is going to take each element and *fold* it into some result—in this case, a `sum`. The result of the fold will be a `Future[Int]`, which will resolve to the `sum`, assuming that the stream eventually terminates.

And, like with a source, sometimes these simple methods are too simple and you need something more complex. In this case, you can fall back to the Graph DSL:

```
class Printer extends GraphStage[SinkShape[Int]] {
  private val in: Inlet[Int] = Inlet("NumberSink")
  override val shape: SinkShape[Int] = SinkShape(in)

  override def createLogic(inheritedAttributes: Attributes): GraphStageLogic = {
    new GraphStageLogic(shape) {
      override def preStart(): Unit = {
        pull(in)
      }

      setHandler(in, new InHandler {
        override def onPush(): Unit = {
```

```
            println(grab(in))
            pull(in)
          }
      })
    }
  }
}
```

This code implements a custom `SinkShape`. It contains a single `Inlet`. Similar to the source example, this inlet represents the input to the stage. It will be connected to the upstream elements. This example uses a `SinkShape`, which is a shape with just a single inlet (Figure 5-9), but again there are more complex shapes that you can use that provide multiple inlets.

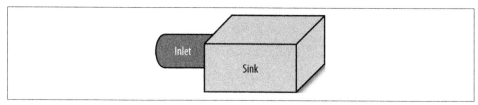

Figure 5-9. A sink

The logic here is very simple: an `InHandler` and its corresponding `onPush` method. The `onPush` method is called when data is pushed into the stream. To access that data, you can call `grab`, which returns the next element. And when you're ready to request more data, you can call `pull`. This signals to the upstream elements that you are ready to accept more data.

To initiate the flow of data, you need to indicate demand. You do that here by overriding the `preStart` method and calling `pull`.

RunnableGraph

A `RunnableGraph` is the result of connecting a source and a sink together. These two things give you the minimal complete system. After you have a `RunnableGraph`, the data can begin moving. Until you have both, you can't do anything. Either you lack a source for the data or you lack a destination. One way or the other, your system is incomplete.

For a graph to be complete, each outlet must be connected to exactly one inlet, as demonstrated in Figure 5-10. If any inlets or outlets remain unconnected, the graph is incomplete and cannot function.

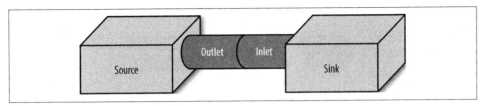

Figure 5-10. RunnableGraph

From the plumbing perspective, a `RunnableGraph` occurs when you connect your water source to your sink (Figure 5-11). Now the water can flow freely from one place to the other. Until you make that connection, you are either pumping water and spraying it out the end of the pump with no real destination, or you have a sink and no water to put in it.

Figure 5-11. Plumbing graph

Flow

As already mentioned, simply connecting your source and your sink is enough to create a runnable flow but it's not really that useful. You are basically just taking the data from one place and putting it into another place without any modification or change. Sometimes, this is desirable, but more commonly you are going to want to perform an operation on that data. You'll want to transform it in some way. This is the purpose of a flow. A flow is a "connector" in which you can transform the data (Figure 5-12). There are many different kinds of flows. Some might modify the data coming from the Source. Others might reduce the data by filtering it or by only taking a portion of it. Flows are connected between the source and the sink. They take your basic `Runna bleFlow` and enhance it, giving it more functionality.

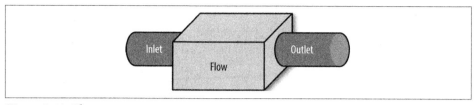

Figure 5-12. Flow

Referring back to our plumbing analogy, a flow is your pipes. You have a source and you have a sink, but it is unrealistic to think that you can simply attach the two with a single length of pipe. Typically, you need to transport the water over some distance. As Figure 5-13 demonstrates, you probably need to change directions a few times. The pipes might become narrower or wider in order to change the pressure. All of these things happen using pipes of various shapes and sizes. Each of these pipes represents a flow.

Figure 5-13. Plumbing flow

Junctions

As your data moves through the system, you might find it necessary to branch out and send portions of it down different paths. Or, it might be necessary to take data from multiple sources and combine it in some way. This is accomplished by using a junction. A junction is basically a branch point. It can be either a fan-in or a fan-out. You can either take a single flow and branch it into many, or combine many flows into one, as shown in Figure 5-14. When you begin using junctions, you are no longer dealing with a simple stream: you are dealing with a *graph*.

Junctions are created as graph elements with multiple inlets or multiple outlets.

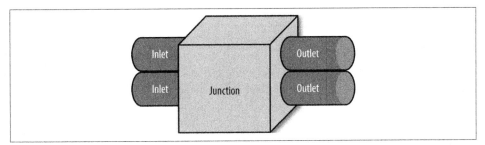

Figure 5-14. A junction

In the plumbing analogy, junctions are represented by things like T-joints and manifolds. They take the water flow coming from the source and branch it to go to multiple different houses, each with its own sink. Or, they might take hot water and cold water and combine them to give us warm water.

Akka Streams give us the means to use combinations of sources, sinks, flows, and junctions to create complex systems called graphs, such as the one depicted in Figure 5-15.

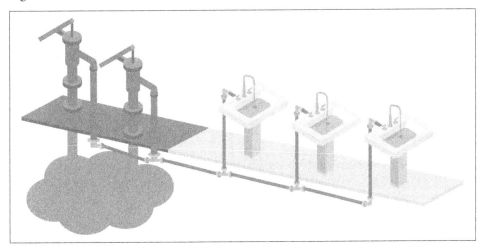

Figure 5-15. A complex graph

Back Pressure in Akka Streams

Akka Streams is built on the concept of back pressure. In this case, the back pressure is implemented by using a push–pull mechanism. When a source and a sink are connected to form a runnable flow, a message is sent from the sink back through the various flows to the source. The message is basically saying that the sink can accept more data. When the source receives this message, it knows that it can send more data to the sink. When data becomes available, the source will pass it through the flows into the sink.

The source is allowed to send only as much data as the sink has requested. If the source receives data and the sink has not requested any, the source must decide what to do with it. It will need to either stash it somewhere or discard it. This might mean that the source simply doesn't draw any more data from the database or file, or it may mean that it must stash or drop a request. This sounds a bit like we have simply moved our overflow problem, not solved it; instead of the overflow happening at the end of the pipe, we have just pushed it up to the beginning of the pipe.

Initially that sounds bad, but when you think about it, that's the best case. At the beginning of the pipe, we are likely far more able to control the data flow and recover from any issues. In most cases, if your system is overloaded, it is likely going to be preferable to block a single user, rather than accepting all requests and then crashing the entire system when it runs out of memory. In the former case, a single user is affected in a very controllable fashion. In the latter case, all users might be affected, and how they are affected could be very nondeterministic.

At the end of the day, with a limited amount of hardware, it is impossible to continue to accept all data no matter how fast it is pushed into the system. At some point, you need to put pressure back on the input to slow down. This is what Akka Streams enables. It forces that pressure back to the entry point into the system. It provides the necessary mechanisms so that when the system experiences excessive load, you can communicate the need to slow down back to the source, which is the only place where we are truly equipped to deal with it.

Using Akka Streams

So how do Akka Streams apply in the real world? Where can we use them? What do they allow us to do? Let's have a look at the scheduling domain for a more concrete example.

Imagine a situation in which someone in the business wants to do some analysis of the data in the system. To do this analysis, she needs to get access to the schedules for a number of different users. She would like those schedules in a JSON format so that the schedules can be fed into another application that will actually perform the analysis. This is a fairly standard Extract, Transform, and Load (ETL) process. We extract the data from one data source, transform it, and then load it into another data source. It's also an excellent candidate for Akka Streams.

Now, in our use case, the person coming with this request has only the email addresses of the people whose data she wants. She doesn't have the actual IDs. Those will need to be looked up. This can be done by using a `PersonRepository`, which looks like this:

```
trait PersonRepository {
  def findByEmail(emailAddress: EmailAddress): Future[Person]
}
```

This code is going to live in a separate bounded context from some of our other services. So the `PersonApi` is going to need to communicate with those other bounded contexts in some manner. This is a scenario for which we might want to use a clustered actor system, or, alternatively, we might choose to use something like Akka Http to expose this data through a REST API. In either case, the `PersonRepository` trait acts as an insulating layer that hides the exact implementation details.

After we have a `Person`, we can obtain the `PersonId`, and we can then use that to find the `Schedule` details. For this, we will make use of a `ScheduleRepository`, which looks like this:

```
trait ScheduleRepository {
  def find(personId: PersonId): Future[Schedule]
}
```

Again, as with the `PersonRepository`, the `ScheduleRepository` is communicating with a separate bounded context. That context is likely not the same as the one with which the `PersonRepository` was communicating. After all, scheduling probably has no need to know about things like email addresses. However, for the report that we are building, we need to have access to information from both contexts. Generating this report is going to involve pulling the data from the necessary sources and then transforming it into the required JSON format.

The input data is going to be just a series of email address strings. However, our trait uses a case class that represents an email address, so we will need to perform a transformation. We can create a flow that will do that for us:

```
val toEmailAddress = Flow[String].map(str => EmailAddress(str))
```

After we have the `EmailAddress`, we'll need to do a lookup on the `PersonRepository` to find the person associated with that email. We can use another flow for this:

```
val findPerson = Flow[EmailAddress].mapAsync(parallelism)(email =>
  personRepository.findByEmail(email))
```

In this case, because the `PersonRepository` returns a future, the flow can't be a simple map operation. Instead, we will use the `mapAsync` operation, which will operate over a future.

After we have a person, we will need to obtain the schedule for that person:

```
val findSchedule = Flow[Person].mapAsync(parallelism)(person =>
  scheduleRepository.find(person.id))
```

And finally, after we have the `Schedule`, we need to do one final operation that will serialize the schedule to JSON format. This might look like the following:

```
val toJson = Flow[Schedule].map(schedule => serializer.toJson(schedule))
```

When all of the pieces are in place, we can stitch it all together into our stream:

```
Source(emailStrings)
  .via(toEmailAddress)
  .via(findPerson)
  .via(findSchedule)
  .via(toJson)
  .runForeach(json => println(json))
```

In this simple example, we are just printing the JSON, but instead of printing, we might send that JSON to another API, or write it to a file, or save it to a database.

Running this will pull our email address strings and run them through the full stream, finally sending them on to their destination. This will all be done in a way that supports back pressure so that we don't overload any aspect of the system. If our findSchedule flow happens to be a bottleneck, we won't allow it to overflow because the back pressure will prevent that. At the same time, we can take advantage of the asynchronous nature of this system. While the findSchedule method is waiting to return, we can continue to process data further upstream or further downstream. We can continue to perform the faster findPerson lookups so that when we are ready to do the next findSchedule, there is already data waiting. We can also continue to perform the toJson operations as long as we have data for them.

At some point, if the findSchedule process is slow enough, something is going to end up waiting. The toJson process will run out of data to process or the back pressure will force us to stop consuming our emailStrings. This is the nature of slow operations. But until that happens, we will make the most of the resources we have available.

Conclusion

Now that you have seen how well-formed actors can be integrated into a system that supports a good flow of data, while maintaining back pressure and reliability, in Chapter 6 we will dig a bit deeper into the specifics of maintaining the right level of data consistency while not impacting the ability to scale.

This is a delicate balance, and relies heavily on the correct construction of actors in the model and a proper integration of those actors, as we have outlined.

Consistency and Scalability

Consistency is a complex attribute of a system, and the need for it varies depending on the system in question. It is very frequently misunderstood, so let's first look at what we mean by consistency before we examine ways to control it.

A system can be said to be *consistent* if different pieces of related data throughout the system are in agreement with one another about the state of the world.

For a simple example, if I calculate the total amount of deposits I've made to a bank account as well as the total number of withdrawals, the system would be *consistent* if it reports a bank balance that agrees with the delta between these two numbers.

On a classic single-processor, single-memory-space von Neumann system, this kind of consistency is not difficult to achieve, in general. Or course, this is assuming that our system doesn't have any bugs.

As soon as a system has any aspect of parallelism, however, consistency becomes a bit more difficult. If we introduce multiple cores, we have some parallelism. If we make the system distributed, the situation becomes even more complex.

As we explained in Chapter 1, the real world doesn't actually have a globally consistent state, so perhaps it's acceptable if our software systems don't either.

In this chapter, we talk about what a transaction means in the context of a distributed system, what the tradeoffs are on consistency, and why global consistency is not the friend of a scalable system. We'll talk about message delivery guarantees and how to avoid the enemies of scalability.

Transactions and Consistency

A transaction in the sense of consistency is considered a single atomic change. This means that the values involved in the change are all updated at once or not at all— there is no point at which some values are changed and some others are not, at least not externally. Of course, in a distributed system this can be a challenge.

The classic example of this is a database *transaction*, during which several tables are updated in a single inviolable unit, but there are many other examples.

As we discuss consistency, we'll see how it applies in Akka's situation.

Strong Versus Eventual Consistency

Data updated via a transaction, in a single atomic instant, is considered to be immediately consistent; that is, the overall system goes from one point at which it is fully consistent to another state in which it is also fully consistent (but with the change). There is no period of time when different parts of the system might have a differing view on the state of the world.

Eventual consistency, on the other hand, implies an update that happens over a span of time, no matter how short that span might be, whereby two different parts of the system might, for a moment, have different opinions on the state of the world. They must come into agreement at some point in the future, but that's the "eventually" part. Consistency is attained, just not instantaneously.

Strangely enough, eventual consistency is usually much easier to achieve than immediate consistency, especially in a distributed environment.

Concurrency Versus Parallelism

Concurrency means that two processes start at some points in time, and their progress overlaps at other points during their processing. This could mean that we start one process, then stop, then start the other, work for a while, stop and start the first again, and so forth. It does not necessarily require the processes to be happening at the same time, just to overlap.

Parallelism, however, introduces the idea of simultaneous progress between two processes; in other words, at least a part of the two (or more) processes are happening in exactly the same time interval. Parallelism implies concurrency, but not the reverse: you can be concurrent without being parallel.

A distributed system is, by definition, parallel, whereas even a single-core, single-processor system can be concurrent by switching which task it's working on over time until both are complete.

Why Globally Consistent Distributed State Doesn't Scale

Aside from the violation of the law of causality in the real world, globally consistent distributed state is very difficult to even approach, much less achieve.

Setting aside whether it is even desirable, let's assume that we want globally consistent distributed state. When we update that state, we need all nodes that are influenced by it (e.g., they have a copy of the data or some data derived from it, such as our bank balance) to have exactly the same opinion as to the state of the world at the moment the update is done.

This effectively means that we need a "stop the world" situation when state is updated, during which some relevant portion of each system is examined and potentially updated to the correct state, and then we can resume processing on all the nodes.

What if one node becomes unavailable during this process? How do we even agree on "now" between nodes (and, no, wall-clock time won't do it). These are difficult problems, that in and of themselves could take a separate book to explore.

The mechanisms to do this in a distributed environment begin to consume a significant part of the resources of the system as a whole, and this gets worse as the size of the distributed group grows. At the same time, during the periods when we are updating state, each node must avoid computing with that state until they all agree on its new value, severely limiting our ability to do processing in parallel, and thus our scalability.

Location Transparency

Location transparency is the feature of a system by which we can perform computations without being concerned with the location (e.g., the node) at which the computation occurs.

In Akka, the flow of messages between actors should be, to the developer, location transparent; that is, we should not care when we send a message whether the recipient is on the same node as the sender. The system itself moves messages across the network as needed to the correct location, without our direct involvement.

Delivery Guarantees

Delivery guarantees are an often-overlooked part of building distributed systems. We frequently consider them when using some communication mechanisms, but we ignore them when using others. When sending a message via an event bus we are careful to consider the delivery guarantee provided by that message bus, but when we send via an HTTP request, we often don't think too much about it. We assume that the message will be delivered, and if it is delivered we will get a successful response. No response means no delivery. And yet, that is not the case.

The delivery guarantees provided by a system are important because they can have a dramatic impact on the consistency of that system. There are three basic types of delivery guarantees that can be defined, but in reality only two of them are actually achievable. The third can be approximated only by using various techniques, which we'll explore later—in the meantime, let's look at the other two.

At Most Once

At Most Once delivery is the simplest guarantee to achieve. It requires no storage, either in memory or on disk, of the messages on either end of the pipeline. This delivery guarantee means that when you send a message, you have no idea whether it will arrive, but that's OK. With this delivery guarantee you must accept the possibility that the message might be lost and thus design around that.

At Most Once delivery simply means that you send the message and then move on. There is no waiting for an acknowledgment. This is the default delivery guarantee in Akka. When a message is sent to an actor using Akka, there is no guarantee that the message will be received. If the actor is local, you can probably assume that it will be delivered, as long as the system doesn't fail, but if the system does fail before the actor can remove the message from the mailbox, that message will be lost. Remember, message processing is asynchronous, so just because the message has been sent does not mean it has been delivered.

Things become even more complicated if the actor is a remote or clustered actor. In this case, you need to deal with the possibility of the remote actor system crashing and losing the message, but you must also consider the possibility that the message might be lost due to a network problem. Regardless of whether the actor is local or remote, the message might not be delivered. If the delivery of the message is critical, you will need to try to work toward an alternative delivery guarantee.

At Least Once

At Least Once delivery is more difficult to achieve in any system. It requires storage of the message on the sender as well as an acknowledgment from the receiver. This storage might be in memory or it might be on disk depending on how important that message delivery is. If the delivery absolutely must succeed, you need to ensure that it is stored somewhere reliable; otherwise you could lose it if the sender fails.

Whether you are storing in memory or on disk, the basic process is to store the message, and then send it and wait for an acknowledgment. If no acknowledgment is received, you resend the message, and continue to do so until you successfully receive an acknowledgment.

With an At Least Once delivery guarantee, there is the possibility of receiving the message twice. If the acknowledgment is lost, when you send the message again, you will have a duplicate delivery. However, because you continue to send until you receive the acknowledgment, you are always guaranteed to get the message at least once, eventually. This delivery mechanism is reliable.

In Akka, you can implement At Least Once delivery a few ways. The first way is to do it manually. In this case, you simply store the message in a queue somewhere, send it, and then expect a response. When the response comes back, you remove the message from the queue. You also need a recovery mechanism so that if the response is never received, you can resend the message.

You can implement this easily in memory by using the Ask pattern. In this case, it might look something like the following:

```scala
class MySender(receiver: ActorRef) extends Actor {
  import context.dispatcher
  implicit val askTimeout = Timeout(5.seconds)

  sendMessage(Message("Hello"))

  private def sendMessage(message: Message):Future[Ack] = {
    (receiver ? message).mapTo[Ack].recoverWith {
    case ex: AskTimeoutException => sendMessage(message)
    }
  }

  override def receive: Receive = Actor.emptyBehavior
}
```

This is a very trivial example—you send a message, and then in the event of an Ask TimeoutException, you try resending it. Of course, this type of delivery is only reliable as long as the sender doesn't crash. If it does, this is not going give you the At Least Once delivery guarantee.

You could adapt the solution that we just described, introducing some database or reliable disk storage. However, it turns out that Akka Persistence has all of this logic built in and provides an AtLeastOnceDelivery trait that you can use for this exact purpose, as shown in the code that follows:

```scala
case class SendMessage(message: String)
case class MessageSent(message: String)

case class AcknowledgeDelivery(deliveryId: Long, message: String)
case class DeliveryAcknowledged(deliveryId: Long)

object MySender {
  def props(receiver: ActorRef) = Props(new MySender(receiver))
}
```

```scala
class MySender(receiver: ActorRef) extends PersistentActor
  with AtLeastOnceDelivery {
  override def persistenceId: String = "PersistenceId"

  override def receiveRecover: Receive = {
    case MessageSent(message) =>
      deliver(receiver.path)(deliveryId =>
        AcknowledgeDelivery(deliveryId, message))
    case DeliveryAcknowledged(deliveryId) =>
      confirmDelivery(deliveryId)
  }

  override def receiveCommand: Receive = {
    case SendMessage(message) => persist(MessageSent(message)) { request =>
      deliver(receiver.path)(deliveryId =>
        AcknowledgeDelivery(deliveryId, message))
    }
    case ack: DeliveryAcknowledged => persist(ack) { ack =>
      confirmDelivery(ack.deliveryId)
    }
  }
}
```

This is a simple implementation of an actor that uses the `AtLeastOnceDelivery` mechanism. Note that it extends `PersistentActor` with `AtLeastOnceDelivery`. This actor will receive a command in the form of `SendMessage`. When the actor receives this command, it sends the message to another actor, but here you want to guarantee delivery. Delivery is guaranteed by persisting the message prior to sending it, and then using the `deliver` method rather than the standard `tell`. When you use the `deliver` method, a delivery ID is generated, which you need to include in the outgoing message (in this case, `AcknowledgeDelivery`).

When the receiving actor gets the resulting message, including the delivery ID, it responds to the sender with another message that contains that same delivery ID (in this case, `MessageAcknowledged`):

```scala
sender() ! MessageAcknowledged(deliveryId)
```

The sender receives and persists the acknowledgment, and simultaneously confirms delivery, as shown in Figure 6-1.

In Figure 6-1, you can see how the sender stores outbound messages and then checks them against `DeliveryAcknowledged`, at which point the outbound message is confirmed to be delivered and no longer needs to be stored.

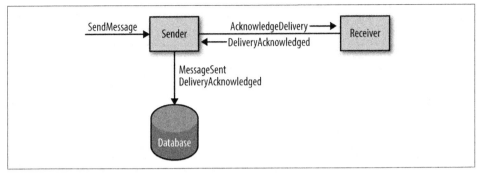

Figure 6-1. Message flow for At Least Once delivery

Under the hood, the actor has a configurable timer. If it does not receive the acknowledgment within the allotted time, it will automatically attempt redelivery.

So, what happens if the sender fails? In the event of a failure, the sender will replay the persisted messages and their corresponding acknowledgments when it is restarted. However, unlike with a standard persistent actor, there is a buffering mechanism in place. During the replay, the messages are not resent immediately. Instead, they are buffered. After all messages have been replayed, the sender can then go through the buffer and compare the delivery requests against the confirmations. It will cross off all the messages that have a corresponding acknowledgment. Then, the sender will resend any messages that are left.

This means that if the receiver fails, or the acknowledgment is lost, the timeout will ensure that the message is redelivered. If the sender fails before it can receive the acknowledgment, when it is restored it will see that no acknowledgment was received and will resend the message. This guarantees that the message will be delivered despite any failures.

Exactly Once Doesn't Exist (But Can Be Approximated)

In many cases, the delivery guarantee that you want is an Exactly Once guarantee. That is, you want each message to be delivered to the destination exactly once, no more, no less. Unfortunately, this type of delivery is impossible to achieve in any system. Instead, you need to strike a balance that uses the delivery guarantees that you can achieve.

Let's consider a very simple example. In our domain, there are multiple bounded contexts. There's a bounded context responsible for updating information on the people in the system, and there's the scheduling bounded context that is responsible for managing the allocation of those people. If you need to delete or deactivate a person (perhaps they have moved to another company), you will need to update both systems. Of course, you want both systems to agree on whether the person is in the system and what the person's allocation looks like. The simple solution seems to be to update one system and have it send a message to the other to perform the appropriate action.

So, the people information system is updated to remove a specific person. That system then sends a message to the scheduling system to remove that person. It is important that this message is delivered, so you wait for an acknowledgment. But what if the acknowledgment never comes? What if there is a network partition while the people information system was trying to send the message? How do you recover? You could assume the message never made it through and send it again. But if the message did get through and it was the acknowledgment that was lost, resending the message would result in a duplicate delivery. On the other hand, if you assume that the message has been received and don't resend it, you run the risk of never delivering the message. Any way you look at it, there is no way to guarantee that the message was delivered exactly once.

But Exactly Once delivery is often what you want. You need to find a way to simulate it.

How Do You Approximate Exactly Once Delivery?

The guarantee that many developers and designers *think* they want is Exactly Once; that is, a message is delivered reliably from the sender to the receiver exactly one time, with no duplications.

In practice, Exactly Once delivery is still impossible, but it is possible to achieve something close to Exactly Once processing, but only by means of an underlying mechanism that abstracts away the problem for us. Under the covers, that solution will be using a mechanism that provides At Least Once delivery to make it appear at the high level that you have Exactly Once processing, at least from the programmer's perspective.

The developer can then send a message via this Exactly Once abstraction and rely on the underlying mechanism to transmit the message, receive an acknowledgment, retransmit if needed, and so forth until the message has been confirmed as received, deduplicated for any repetition on the receiving side, and finally, delivered to the recipient. Of course, this process can affect performance, especially if many retransmissions must occur before the confirmation can be made. It also definitely requires persistence, at least on the sender's side, and often on both the sender and receiver's side.

It is often desirable to have more visibility to the underlying mechanism, so it is fairly uncommon in Akka systems to see an abstraction to simulate Exactly Once.

Cluster Singleton

Sometimes, there are areas within a system that by necessity must be unique. Creating multiple copies is unacceptable because these areas of the system might have state that must be very tightly controlled. An example of this would be a unique ID generator. A unique ID generator might need to keep track of previously used IDs. Or, it might use a monotonically increasing number value. In either case, it might be critical that you ensure that only a single call to generate an ID happens at any given time. Trying to generate IDs in parallel could perhaps result in duplicates.

An ID generator such as in this example is a bottleneck in the system and should be avoided whenever possible. But sometimes there are situations for which it is necessary. In this case, Akka provides a facility for ensuring that only a single instance of an actor is available throughout a clustered system. This is done through an Akka *cluster singleton*.

A cluster singleton works by having the singleton always run on the oldest available node in the cluster. Determining which node is the oldest is done via the actor system's gossip mechanism. After the cluster has established the oldest node, the singleton instance of the actor can be instantiated on that node. All of this is handled behind the scenes through the use of a cluster singleton manager. This manager will take care of the details of ensuring the singleton is running.

There is a wrapper actor around the singleton called the *cluster singleton proxy*. This proxy is used to communicate with the singleton. All messages are passed through the proxy, and it is the job of the proxy to determine to which node to send the message. Again, where that singleton lives is transparent to clients. They need know only about an instance of the proxy, and the details are handled under the hood.

But what happens if the node hosting the singleton is lost? In this case, there will be a period of time during which that singleton is unavailable. In the meantime, the cluster will need to reestablish which node is the oldest and reinitialize the singleton on that node. During this period of unavailability, any messages sent to the cluster singleton proxy will be buffered. As soon as the singleton becomes available again, the messages will be delivered. If those messages had a timeout associated with them, it is possible that they will timeout before the singleton is reestablished.

One of the big disadvantages of the singleton pattern is that you cannot guarantee availability. There is simply no way to ensure that there is always a node available. There will always be a transition period from when the singleton is lost to when it is reestablished. Even though that period might be short in many cases, it still represents a potential failure in the system.

Another disadvantage to the singleton pattern is that it is a bottleneck. Because there can be only one instance of the actor, it can process only one message at a time. This means that the system could be stuck waiting for long periods while it works its way through a backlog.

Another potential issue is that when the singleton is migrated from one node to the next, any state stored in the singleton is lost. It will then be necessary to re-create that state when the singleton is reestablished. One way to do this would be to use Akka Persistence to maintain that state. In that case, it will be automatically restored when the singleton is re-created.

Because of the disadvantages of the cluster singleton pattern, it is recommended that you avoid it, except when absolutely necessary. And when it is necessary, you should keep it as small as possible. For example, if you were using the singleton to generate unique user IDs, it would be best if that was all it did. Although it might be tempting to have the singleton create the users in the database and initialize their state, each additional operation the singleton needs to perform creates a bigger bottleneck. If you can limit it to a single operation, ideally in memory, you can ensure that you are keeping it as available as possible.

Here is an example of what a very simple ID generator might look like if it were implemented using Akka Persistence:

```
object IdProvider {
  case object GenerateId
  case class IdGenerated(id: Int)

  def props() = Props(new IdProvider)
}

class IdProvider extends PersistentActor {
  import IdProvider._

  override val persistenceId: String = "IdProvider"

  private var currentId = 0

  override def receiveRecover: Receive = {
    case IdGenerated(id) =>
      currentId = id
  }

  override def receiveCommand: Receive = {
    case GenerateId =>
      persist(IdGenerated(currentId + 1)) { evt =>
        currentId = evt.id
        sender() ! evt
      }
  }
}
```

The `IdProvider` class is very simple. It takes a single message, `GenerateId`, and returns a result `IdGenerated`. The actor itself, upon receiving a `GenerateId` command, will create an `IdGenerated` event, persist that event, update the current ID, and then send the event back to the sender.

When the `IdProvider` is re-created, in the event of a failure, it will playback all the previous messages using the `receiveRecover` behavior, restoring its state in the process, so nothing will have been lost. It will then continue to generate IDs on the recovered node as though there were no interruption.

This `IdProvider` is in no way related to Akka Cluster. This code could be used in any actor system, whether it is clustered or not. This is an example of how location transparency can be a benefit. You could build your system under the assumption that this will be a local actor, and later, when you decide to make it a clustered actor, this code doesn't need to change.

After you have decided that you want to cluster this actor and in fact make it into a singleton, you can do that with very little actual code. To cluster this actor, use the following:

```
val singletonManager = system.actorOf(ClusterSingletonManager.props(
    singletonProps = IdProvider.props(),
    terminationMessage = PoisonPill,
    settings = ClusterSingletonManagerSettings(system)),
  name = "IdProvider"
)
```

This is creating the instance of the `ClusterSingletonManager`. This manager must be created on any nodes on which you might want to host the singleton. It will then ensure that the singleton is created on one of those nodes.

You don't send messages through the manager; to send messages to the actor, you need to create a `ClusterSingletonProxy`. To create a proxy, use the following:

```
val idProvider = system.actorOf(ClusterSingletonProxy.props(
    singletonManagerPath = "/user/IdProvider",
    settings = ClusterSingletonProxySettings(system)),
  name = "IdProvider")
```

This proxy takes a path to the actor. What you get back is an `ActorRef`, but that `Actor Ref` will now proxy to the singleton, wherever it might be. You can use this `ActorRef` just like any other `ActorRef` in the system. Again, this demonstrates the power of location transparency. Any actors that previously were sending messages to a local `ActorRef` can now be given this proxy instead. They don't need to know that the proxy is now a cluster singleton actor. They can continue to operate as though the actor were local, and the bulk of the code remains unchanged. The only place in the code where you do need to make changes is in the construction of the actor. Rather than constructing a local actor, you are now constructing the cluster singleton proxy. That's it.

Scalability

Scalability refers to the ability of a system to handle higher load without failure or sharp degradation in performance. It is only tangentially related to performance, and optimizing performance is no guarantee of scalability (and vice versa).

Increasing performance means that your system can respond *faster* to the *same* load, whereas scalability is more concerned with the system's reaction to *higher* load, whether that is more simultaneous requests, a larger dataset, or simply a higher rate of requests.

Figure 6-2 graphs the response time under increasing load for a system. The graph shows that a system that fails to scale will tend to have an inflection point where it either fails (wholly or partially) and some requests are not handled, or where it begins to rapidly decline in performance; that is, the response time for each request goes up rapidly with increasing load. The latter will usually also result in failure at some point —the client will often time out when the response time is too long.

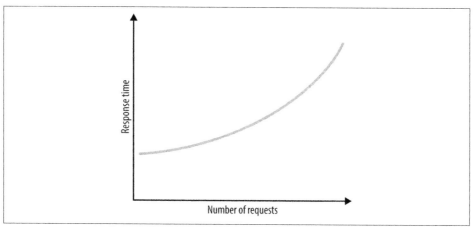

Figure 6-2. Response time versus number of requests

A system with increased *performance* will move the response-time line *down* (indicating a faster response time) without moving anything else, as depicted in Figure 6-3.

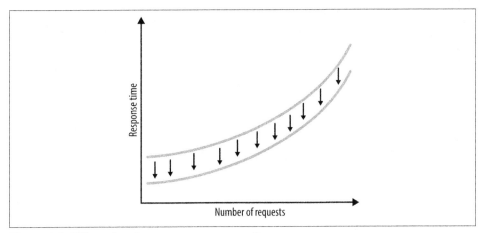

Figure 6-3. Effect of performance on response time

A system that increases its *scalability*, however, moves the entire curve to the right; that is, the point of diminishing returns indicated by the response times increasing sharply toward an unacceptable amount doesn't occur until the system is under higher load. As Figure 6-4 demonstrates, the performance need not change at all (although some degree of coupling between these two is normal).

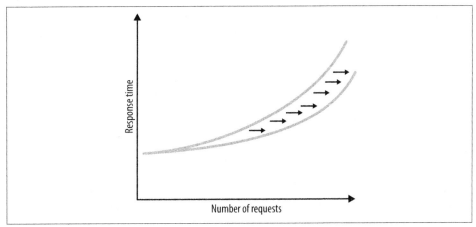

Figure 6-4. Effect of scalability on the number of requests

Systems tend to scale along two axes: horizontal and vertical. Vertical scalability means if you run your system on a larger machine with more resources (CPU capability, memory, and so on), you can handle a higher load. This is usually easier, but is not a given—some systems don't benefit much by this, because they become bound by constraints other than CPU and memory, so increasing them doesn't help beyond a certain point.

The horizontal axis, on the other hand, is of much more interest. This is when you add additional systems or nodes to your group of nodes that comprise the entire system. By doing so, you gain the ability to handle more load. Often, scaling out this way doesn't result in any performance gain: the system continues to handle each request on average in about the same amount of time—it's just that you have the ability to handle more of them.

Let's take a very very simple compute problem, adding two integers, and think about its scalability.

On a single system, adding more compute and memory might buy you a bit, until you hit the maximum number of incoming requests—let's assume, as is often the case, that requests come in over the network in some fashion. You will likely run out of network bandwidth at some point on the scale of increasing volume of requests, no matter how many integers the system can add and no matter the speed.

This problem, however, scales out horizontally really well. By adding a second machine, the system can handle roughly twice as many requests in the same period. In this super-simple example of adding two integers, the only potential point of commonality in the group of servers you are building would be in request routing—for example, a network switch or load balancer, perhaps—and such units can be scaled quite effectively.

We are starting with what is known as a *share nothing* architecture; that is, our nodes don't share any information at all with each other—they just add integers, return the result, and are ready for the next request.

As the computational demands on the system grow, however, the picture of course changes. As soon as there is a need for the nodes to share state, no matter how straightforward, the possibility of introducing a bottleneck arises. Let's say, to keep it simple, that you want to count how many requests the system has processed in total and make this number available via some kind of API.

The total requests for the cluster is a surprisingly complex computational problem. For example, when is this total incremented? Is it at the end of the request or at the beginning? If the total is continually accurate, you have a need for global state, which, as we've already discussed, is the root of many problems in a distributed system. It's easy enough to think about computing the requests on a single node (although even this has a microcosm of the same issues), but as soon as you add a second machine, you add a difficult problem.

In distributed systems, and in Akka in particular, eventual consistency and the Actor Model are the way that you can approach this problem. Instead of trying to have a single up-to-the-instant total of the number of requests, you should opt for an eventually consistent number on each node and an eventually consistent total for the cluster. In the Actor Model, you would likely send a message to an accumulator actor on each node for each request, and then have that accumulator report the totals in turn to a cluster singleton accumulator. The cluster singleton accumulator would then have a view on the number of requests that is being updated constantly, but would always lag in reality by a short (and likely irrelevant) interval.

Handling such a count is actually a good use case for monitoring, which is a different flavor of computation designed to allow near-real-time visualization of the operation of a system—in this case, a distributed system.

In cases of high load, you likely wouldn't have each computing actor (e.g., the ones adding the two numbers) report *every* request. Instead, you would probably hold a count for a few requests and report every 100 or so (unless there are no requests for a short interval) to keep the message volume more manageable. You might want to consider allowing the "rollup" count to vary, depending on load. This way, when the load is low, the system reports every request or two, but under higher volume, it reports only every 100 or every 1,000.

As you can see, it can become surprisingly complicated in a short period of time, but following the pattern of the Actor Model in general prevents you from doing things that are simply not suitable to high scale.

The key portions of the definition of scalability are "without failure" and "degradation in performance," so let's examine each of these in turn.

The "without failure" portion implies that even as the load increases, the system won't suddenly give up and fail to handle requests. It should "degrade in performance," ideally in a nonabrupt manner, as resources become fully consumed on the cluster.

These two go hand in hand, because when a portion of an Actor Model system fails, it should not affect other parts. This means that from the client's point of view—the client being the component that is sending all these numbers—nothing broke, even though one or more of your actors or nodes did in fact have a problem.

If you have enough nodes (and figuring out "enough" is another whole conversation, although it should generally be an absolute minimum of three), the system's performance should decrease slowly as load increases, as some nodes (ideally evenly distributed) become saturated.

A strongly related concept to scalability is *elasticity*. This is the ability to add resources to a running system, thus increasing its ability to scale, all without the clients being affected.

In this scenario, if you can add new nodes to your load-balancer, and those new nodes begin sending statistics to the cluster singleton accumulator, you can achieve this. As the cluster grows, you might get to the point at which the messages to the cluster singleton become the limiting factor, but we discussed the tactic of sending accumulated messages less frequently as a way to compensate.

Even in this relatively trivial example, you can see that monitoring can be very helpful: if you can see, for instance, that the queue length of unprocessed messages for the actor that is rolling up your counts is becoming higher over time, you can use this information to adjust the accumulation factor, providing some simple self-tuning in the system. If you also use the totals as a means to detect when new nodes should be added as load increases, you have achieved one half of elasticity. The other half is the reverse: you also need to be able to scale *down* your cluster when load *decreases*.

If compute resources are a cost, this scaling down can be as important as scaling up, and an elastic system is a significant tool for saving money.

The patterns for building a scalable system generally revolve around a few basic principles, although the application of these principles can be quite sophisticated. Let's take a look at them in the following subsections.

Avoid Global State

If you can avoid *global* state, you will have bypassed the biggest single limiting factor on the scalability of a system. If you *require* such state, you can achieve it using a cluster singleton actor as a wrapper; however, you will be sacrificing scalability by doing this.

Avoid Shared State

Global state is, of course, just the extreme case of any *shared* state; that is, information shared between the nodes of your cluster. If you minimize or ideally eliminate such shared state, many of the obstacles to scalability go away, as well. Failing that, you again isolate the shared state behind an actor, and carefully monitor its impact.

Follow the Actor Model

Building your system entirely in the Actor Model, and not just using actors here and there, allows the maximum flexibility in adapting to the changing load because any portion of the system can be distributed further with the location transparency of actors.

Avoid Sequential Operations

We did not encounter this in our simple example, but many systems with a goal of scalability have the flaw of requiring sequential operations. This is a form of state, and it spans time, as well, which is a double hazard.

If a certain operation cannot be performed until some *other* operation is complete, you are forced to make your actors use something like a finite-state machine (FSM) model to accommodate this, which in many cases severely limits scalability.

Although it is often very difficult to take a design and make its messages not depend on sequence, you can achieve it with some careful design, and it is always worth it from the perspective of scalability (not to mention the simplicity of the system itself usually increases—a pleasant side effect).

Isolate Blocking Operations

Our example didn't include I/O, but this is the usual culprit when introducing blocking operations into any actor-based system. If you must have such operations, again let the Actor Model be your guide, and with Akka, isolate the dispatcher for blocking operations from the dispatcher used for nonblocking operations. This way, you are able to tune them independently. Isolating these operations to another thread pool is key to keeping your application responsive. We will discuss how and where to do this in more detail in Chapter 9 when we discuss dispatchers.

Monitor and Tune

Monitoring a running actor system under load is the only way to truly gauge its behavior because it is by nature nondeterministic, especially when distributed.

Knowing what to monitor and how this should affect your tuning decisions is discussed in other sections of this book, and indeed in many other books. Monitoring is an art worthy of study in and of itself because it can yield significant gains in scalability.

Cluster Sharding and Consistency

In many systems, consistency and scalability are enemies. If you want consistency, you must sacrifice scalability. Consistency requires that nodes in a cluster share information among themselves. This in turn reduces scalability. But it doesn't need to be that way. Akka cluster sharding provides a way to bridge the gap between consistency and scalability within a single concept. It does this by allowing you to create boundaries that control consistency and scalability. But before we delve deeply into how it does that, let's first talk about what sharding is.

Sharding

The concept of sharding has been in use in database systems for a long time. It is a powerful tool that makes it possible to scale and distribute databases, while keeping them consistent. The basic idea is that every record in your database has a *shard key* attached to it. This shard key is used to determine the distribution of data. Rather than storing all records for the database on a single node in the cluster, the records are distributed according to this shard key.

Figure 6-5 depicts a very simple two-shard setup. In this example, you could use a numeric key: all odd-numbered entries would be on one shard (node), whereas all even-numbered entries would be on the other shard (node).

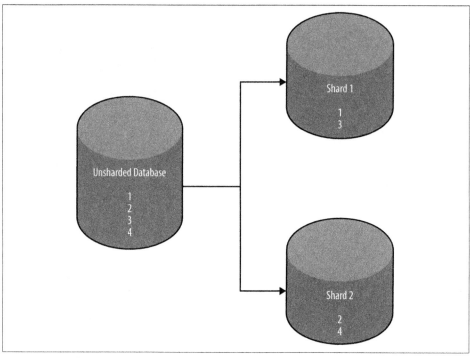

Figure 6-5. Effect of sharding a database

By distributing the records in this way, you reduce contention for the shared resource. It gives you the ability to distribute the load across the nodes in the cluster rather than requiring all requests to go to the same node. This also distributes the consistency requirements. All requests for a specific record will always go to the shard that contains that record. You need to maintain consistency of that record within that shard. However, maintaining consistency among different shards is not required, because they don't share any data.

To enable sharding, there needs to be a reliable way to determine on which shard the data resides. This is often done by using a special node that routes traffic to the appropriate shard. This router doesn't need to do a lot of work; it just keeps track of the shards and routes traffic as necessary. Although it is still a bottleneck in the system, the work it does is trivial, so the effect of that bottleneck is minimized.

Sharding in Akka

Akka cluster sharding takes this idea a step further. Rather than sharding the data, you shard live actors across the cluster. Each actor is assigned an entity ID. This ID is unique within the cluster. It usually represents the identifier for the domain entity that the actor is modeling. You provide a function that will extract that entity ID from the message being sent. You also provide a function that takes the message and computes the ID for the shard on which the actor will reside.

When a message is sent, the aforementioned functions are applied to locate the appropriate shard using the shard ID, and then to locate the actor within that shard using the entity ID (see Figure 6-6). This makes it possible for you to locate the unique instance of that actor within the cluster. In the event that no actor currently exists, the actor will be created. The sharding system will ensure that only one instance of each actor exists in the cluster at any time.

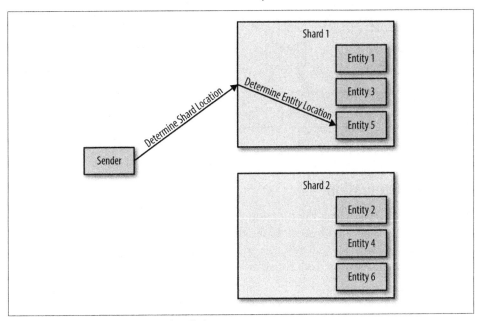

Figure 6-6. Message flow in a sharded system

Shards are distributed across the cluster in what are known as *shard regions*. These regions act as hosts for the shards. Each node that participates in sharding will host a single shard region for each type of sharded actor. Each region can in turn host multiple shards. All entities within a shard region are represented by the same type of actor.

Each individual shard can host many entities. These entities are distributed across the shards according to the computation of the shard ID that you provided.

Internally, a shard coordinator is used to manage where the shards are located. The coordinator informs shard regions as to the location of individual shards. Those shard regions can in turn be used to send a message to the entities hosted by the shards. This coordinator is implemented as a cluster singleton. However, its interaction within the actual message flow is minimized. It only participates in the messaging if the location of the shard is not known. In this case, the shard region can communicate with the shard coordinator to locate the shard. That information is then cached. Going forward, messages can be sent directly without the need to communicate with the coordinator. The caching mechanisms mean that the communication with the coordinator is minimal and as a result it rarely, if ever, becomes a bottleneck. Figure 6-7 presents an overview.

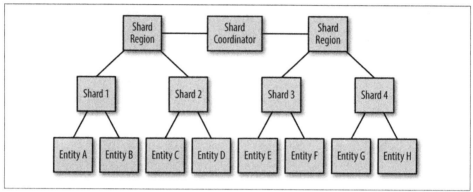

Figure 6-7. Components of cluster sharding

Shard Key Generation

For sharding to be efficient, the function that is used to determine the shard ID must provide a fairly even distribution. If the distribution is poor, you can end up with a situation in which all of the traffic is routed to the same shard, which defeats the entire purpose of sharding. Let's consider a quick example.

In Chapter 2, we talked about the possibility of using the first letter in a person's name as the shard ID. This accommodates 26 shards with actors distributed across these shards. However, this strategy has some serious drawbacks. Certain letters are more common for names. *T*, *S*, and *A*, for example, might be very popular, whereas *Q* or *X* are much less popular. This means that the distribution of shards won't be even. Some shards will have many actors, whereas others will have very few. This can lead to certain nodes in the cluster receiving the bulk of the traffic while other nodes sit idle.

The goal is to have the entity actors be evenly distributed among the shards. A common way to achieve this is to take your entity's unique identifier and compute a numeric hash. This gives you something fairly random, which should allow for a fairly even distribution. This by itself is insufficient, however. Simply computing a numeric hash will result in a very large number of shards. This is usually undesirable. Too many shards can increase the maintenance of the cluster. Thus, you want to reduce the number of possible shards. You can do this by computing the modulo of the hash by the desired number of shards, as shown here:

```
(entityId.hashCode() % maxShards).toString
```

Shard Distribution

So, how do you determine what the appropriate number of shards is? Having too many shards creates a large maintenance burden on the sharding system; having too few can create other issues.

If there are too few shards, it can become impossible to distribute them evenly across the cluster. For example, if you have only two shards in a cluster of three nodes, you will have one node that is doing nothing. This obviously is undesirable. Conversely, if you have four shards in a cluster of three nodes, one node in the cluster will be required to do roughly twice as much work as the others. This, too, is a situation that you want to avoid.

A good rule of thumb is to have at least 10 times the maximum number of cluster nodes. This means that each node in the cluster will be hosting 10 or more shards. This is a good balance. It means that as nodes are added or removed from the cluster, the rebalance of the cluster won't put a significant burden on any single node. The shards can be redistributed evenly across the cluster.

Consistency Boundary

With this basic understanding of how sharding works, how does it help with consistency specifically? Sharding provides a consistency boundary in the form of a single consistent actor in the cluster. All communication that is done with a specific entity ID always goes through that actor. The Akka cluster sharding mechanism ensures that only one actor with the given ID is running in the cluster at any time. This means that you can use the single-threaded illusion to your advantage. You know that any requests will always go to that actor. You also know that actor can process only one message at a time. This means that you can guarantee message ordering and consistent state within the bounds of that actor.

This does create a potential bottleneck, though. As Figure 6-8 illustrates, all requests for a single ID go through the single entity actor assigned to that ID. Thus, if many requests are coming into that actor, the actor becomes a bottleneck. Messages might become backed up in the actor's mailbox if the load is large enough. In practice, though, this almost never manifests as a real problem. As long as you have been careful in deciding which actors to shard, you should be able to easily avoid this bottleneck. And if it should ever manifest itself, it will be isolated to a single entity. All requests for that entity go through the same actor, but all requests for all other entities go through different actors. So, in the event that a flood of messages comes into that actor, it will slow only that ID. All other IDs will not experience issues. In a real-world scenario, if we sharded based on User ID, only a single user would experience the bottleneck; all other users could continue to operate without noticing any issues.

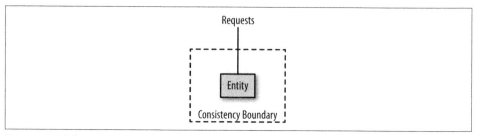

Figure 6-8. The consistency boundary of an entity

This approach yields total consistency for the given entity within the boundary of that actor, but there is a cost to maintaining this consistency that you need to be aware of. According to CAP theorem, you must choose two characteristics from among the three that you'd ideally like to have: consistency, availability, and partition tolerance. You can never have all three. Partition tolerance is not usually something that production systems are willing to sacrifice, which leaves you selecting between consistency and availability. In our case, we have opted for consistency, and as a result we have lost availability. In the event that the node hosting the shard is lost, or a rebalance occurs, there will be a period of time during which the entity actors are unavailable while the shard is being moved to another node. Even though the migration itself is fast, taking only a few seconds, the decision as to whether to migrate is largely dependent on your configured failure-detection mechanisms. Depending on how you have set up failure detection, the migration could be significantly longer.

Scalability Boundary

We have used sharding to enable consistency, but if consistency is the enemy of scalability, how can sharding help? By creating a boundary around the consistency, isolating it to a single entity, you can use that boundary to allow scalability. Consistency is limited to a single entity, and therefore you can scale the system across multiple entities.

When you need to scale the system, you can create new nodes and redistribute the shards across those new nodes, as demonstrated in Figure 6-9. This means that the work that was previously handled by one node can potentially be handled by multiple nodes. This reduces the overall amount of work that any individual node needs to perform, yielding great scalability potential.

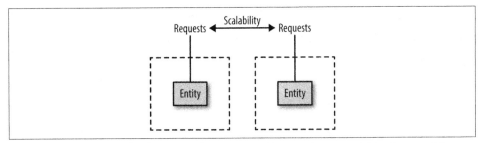

Figure 6-9. Scaling multiple entities but maintaining consistency within those entities

Sharding Aggregate Roots

Sharding relies heavily on our ability to correctly select the proper entities to shard. This requires an understanding of where consistency is required within your domain. So how then do you decide what is a suitable candidate for sharding?

As usual, when deciding where to apply sharding, you should go back to the principles of domain-driven design (DDD). You have already established certain criteria for sharding. The actors must be uniquely identifiable. This means that if you have modeled your actor system after your domain, the actors will be entities in the domain. But we can take it a step further than that.

When sharding, it is often desirable to branch out to the sharded actors based on the entity ID, but then within that entity ID, you often want to keep all operations on the local machine. That is, you use the cluster to locate the sharded actor, but after that you minimize any remote communication. Minimizing the remote communication improves performance because you eliminate the network latency from the equation. It also eliminates the need to serialize and deserialize messages.

Often, a good place to begin looking at sharding is the system's aggregate roots. Aggregate roots often give us a natural consistency boundary within a domain. We usually care that the data within that aggregate is consistent, but across multiple aggregates it is not critical. When performing operations in the domain, you typically touch only a single aggregate root, which means that you can potentially minimize network communication. The bulk of the operation can be performed by the aggregate root, its children, or local services, calling out over the network only when it becomes necessary. By reducing the amount of communication that happens over the network, you improve the efficiency of the operation.

In our project management domain, one of the aggregate roots is a person. This will be a good place for us to investigate sharding. From the perspective of consistency, this provides a lot of benefits. You can guarantee all messages go through a single actor for a single person. This means that you never need to worry about two projects trying to schedule the same person at the same time. This single-entity actor provides a consistency boundary that prevents this from happening. It also gives you a very nice place to provide scalability. You can process multiple people across many different machines, which allows you to distribute the load. The asynchronous, distributed nature of actor systems are a natural fit to provide the consistency and scalability that you need.

Persistence

Distributing the actors in this way means that the sharding system must occasionally perform rebalances. These rebalances mean that any actors that were in memory need to be unloaded from memory. When this happens, you lose any state. The actors might eventually be reestablished in their new home, but you will have lost everything.

There are a number of ways to reestablish this state in the new location, but perhaps the most convenient way is to take advantage of Akka Persistence. Akka Persistence requires that actors be uniquely identifiable. Cluster sharding has the same requirement. This makes it very natural to pair the two. The Persistence ID for the actor becomes the Entity ID.

Akka Persistence provides built-in support for event sourcing. Commands that are sent to the actor are persisted as events in a journal. When the actor is re-created later, it can replay those events to reestablish the previous state. This means that the actor can be unloaded from memory at any time because you can always rebuild the state later from the event journal. You can think of commands as the thing you are asking your actor to do, and the events are the things that the actor has done. There is not necessarily a one-to-one relationship between the commands and events. It is possible for a command to be rejected, resulting in no events. It is also possible for a command to issue multiple events.

With your actor established as persistent, you can ensure that if a rebalance occurs and the actor needs to migrate to another node, when it does so it will be reestablished with all of its state intact. This means that the location of that actor doesn't need to be consistent. It can be flexible as necessary.

Passivation

It is unreasonable to expect that a system will maintain all actors in memory at all times. The presence of persistence means that you no longer need to keep your actors in memory. You can load them and unload them as required, and because they are persistent, when they are loaded again, they will reestablish their state. However, if you simply stop the actor, any messages pending waiting in that actor's mailbox will be lost. A `PoisonPill` allows the mailbox to be drained but doesn't prevent new messages from entering the mailbox after the `PoisonPill`.

To alleviate this, sharding introduces the concept of *passivation*. Rather than simply stopping, an actor can instead passivate. In this case, a message is sent to the shard region, informing it that this specific actor is passivating. This signals the shard region to begin buffering any new messages to that actor. In the meantime, the actor is sent a custom message that is placed in its mailbox. The actor will eventually receive that message and can then shut itself down. If no new messages were buffered by the shard region, the actor will remain shut down. In the event that a new message is received, after the shutdown the actor will be re-created and the new message will be delivered.

Often this is achieved by using the setReceiveTimeout operation within an actor. This operation makes it possible for you to trigger a ReceiveTimeout message if no new messages are received within a given amount of time. When this idle period has elapsed, the actor can then choose to passivate.

Passivation means that when an actor is working hard, all of its state can be kept in memory and it can process new requests very quickly and efficiently. However, when that actor becomes idle, it can be unloaded from memory. When more requests come into the actor, it can be re-created on the first message and then, again, every message after that can operate on the in-memory state, allowing for huge efficiency gains. This basically turns your actor into a write-through cache for the state of that entity.

Using Cluster Sharding for Consistency

Cluster sharding requires a minimal amount of code to use in its most basic form. Without persistence or passivation, any actor can be sharded with a few very simple changes. The main change is in the way that you send a message to the actor. Rather than sending directly to the actor, you need to send it to the shard region. You do this by creating the shard region:

```
val shardRegion: ActorRef = ClusterSharding(system).start(
    typeName = "People",
    entityProps = Person.props(),
    settings = ClusterShardingSettings(system),
    extractEntityId = extractEntityId,
    extractShardId = extractShardId)
```

This example creates a shard region called People. This shard region is going to host actors of type Person. You can see where we have passed the Props to construct a Person so that the shard region will know how to create them. This code also passes the extractEntityId function and the extractShardId function. These allow you to take the incoming message and parse it to extract the necessary shard ID, entity ID, and the actual message.

Again, in the absence of Akka Persistence and passivation, this will work as is. No other changes are necessary. However, a nonpersistent sharded actor is not that useful due to the loss of state that might happen during a rebalance. So what does the actor look like if we want to include persistence and passivation? Let's take a look at it in the following example:

```scala
class Person extends PersistentActor {

  override def persistenceId: String = s"Person-${self.path.name}"

  context.setReceiveTimeout(timeout)

  override def receiveRecover: Receive = {
    case AddToProject(project) =>
      // Update State
  }

  override def receiveCommand: Receive = {
    case AddToProject(project) =>
      persist(AddedToProject(project)) { addedToProject =>
      // Update State
    }
    case ReceiveTimeout =>
      context.parent ! Passivate(PoisonPill)
  }
}
```

This is a very simple stub of what such an actor might look like. It is a very simple persistent actor. The only difference from any other persistent actor is the presence of the `context.setReceiveTimeout(timeout)`. This timeout will cause the actor to receive the `ReceiveTimeout` message if it hasn't seen any new messages within the given timeout. When this occurs, we send the `Passivate(PoisonPill)` to the parent actor. This in turn instructs the host shard region to shut down the actor using a `PoisonPill`. If you want to, you can use a custom shutdown message, which would be delivered to the actor in order to shut it down.

So, what do the `extractEntityId` and `extractShardId` functions look like? This will vary depending on your implementation, but let's have a look at a very simple example.

A common practice when using cluster sharding is to create an envelope message to contain the various pieces necessary for sharding. This envelope is not required. If all of the information is present in the existing message, you can just set up the extractors to pull that information as required. However, if pieces of information are not present, you can wrap the message in an envelope:

```scala
case class Envelope(entityId: EntityId, message: Message)
```

This envelope can take whatever form is best for your particular use case. For this case, the envelope simply gives you the `entityId` and message as separate pieces.

The extractor functions are then trivial to implement:

```
def extractEntityId: ExtractEntityId  = {
  case Envelope(id, message) => (id.toString, message)
}

def extractShardId: ExtractShardId = {
  case Envelope(id, _) => (id.hashCode % maxShards).toString
}
```

ExtractEntityId is actually an alias to a partial function with the signature `Partial Function[Any, (String, Any)]`. These, and other, types of aliases provide better readability to the code. You can see that this function is just extracting the components of the envelope and converting `id` to a string.

ExtractShardId is an alias to a partial function with the signature `PartialFunc tion[Any, String]`. In this case, it is computing the shard `id` and then converting the numeric value to a string.

Again, we emphasize that the envelope and the extractor functions can be as simple or as complex as your use case requires. If your use case requires additional information to be stored in the envelope to compute the shard key, you can add it in. There is nothing special about the structure of that envelope or the extractor functions. You can define them however you like.

In general, though, it is probably best to start simple. Use a very simple envelope (or no envelope at all) and do a minimal amount of work in your extractors. As the complexity of the application grows, you can look at enriching this functionality if necessary.

Using cluster sharding, you can create systems that provide a good balance between consistency and scalability. It can allow you to scale a system to many nodes with relative ease within some clearly defined boundaries. Combined with Akka Persistence and passivation, you can guard against the loss of state or the loss of messages in the event of a rebalance or failure. But you still need to accept the fact that failures can, and will, occur, and although these techniques can help with certain types of failures, they don't cover everything. In Chapter 7, we will look in more detail at the different types of failures our application can experience, and how we can use the principles of Akka to mitigate those failures.

Conclusion

Now that we have discussed the balance of consistency and scalability, and given examples of the appropriate levels of consistency in a distributed system, we will consider the failure cases more closely. What happens when portions of your system fail, and how should your system react?

A highly distributed system is *more* likely to have some portion of the system fail than a single-node system—there are simply more moving parts that can potentially go wrong.

At the same time, however, a properly formed distributed system is far *less* likely to have the *system* as a whole fail, as we will see in Chapter 7.

Fault Tolerance

A common quality among developers is the element of perfectionism. We strive to build software that will be resilient against failure, and often we don't want to admit that failures are a fact of life. The reality is that no matter how much we strive for perfection, there are always going to be elements that are out of our control. Even when we can control it, bugs will creep into the system. No system is perfect. We try to anticipate and predict every possible failure, but the truth is that the possibilities are endless. Even if we could build our software to be perfect, we must plan for hardware failures. And if we do plan for hardware failures, we must consider how network partitions affect our system. What happens when a hurricane wipes out our datacenter? We plan for the situation when every aspect of our software and hardware is behaving perfectly, but an external dependency outside of our control fails.

What might be better is to accept the fact that failures will occur. Instead of trying to handle every possible case, would it not be better to ensure that we can recover properly when the unexpected occurs? This will put us in a better place overall. Rather than trying to see the future and build a perfect system, we should instead try to build a system that is smart enough to deal with the unexpected. It recognizes that failure is a fact of life and embraces it rather than trying to ignore it.

Handling failure is, in many ways, another aspect of letting go of global consistency. Trying to maintain global consistency led us down the path of ignoring time, but it also means ignoring failures. We must assume that when we try to send a message to a system, it might well be unavailable at that moment, and our message might be lost. How can we guarantee consistency in that case? The only option then, in the event of a failed system, is to notify the end user about the error. This avoids the potential inconsistency, but in turn creates a negative user experience. This is the classic trade-off of the CAP theorem. We can't have consistency, availability, and partition tolerance, all at the same time. This typically means sacrificing either consistency or availability.

As with many other aspects of Akka, it is often helpful to think about the system in terms of real people. So let's consider that for a moment. Consider the case of a customer ordering food at a restaurant. We'll view the customer as our end user, and the staff of the restaurant and the tools that they use will be the software we are building. When our customer comes in and orders dinner, she has made a request that she expects to be completed in a timely manner. But what happens in the event of failure?

In traditional software development, we often deal with failure in one of two ways. We either throw an exception, or, if we are doing functional programming, we return a failure value. We then expect the caller of the code to deal with the error or we eventually inform the user of the error. Is that reasonable?

Suppose that after our customer has ordered her meal, the server makes a mistake when communicating to the kitchen, and the order is prepared incorrectly. Should the server go back to the customer and ask her to deal with the problem? It might be desirable to inform the customer that her meal will be delayed, but the customer doesn't need to know all the details, and she definitely can't be expected to do anything about the failure. What if the order was entered correctly, but the cook dropped the food during preparation? Should the cook expect the server to deal with that failure? Is the server even capable of dealing with the problem? In most cases, the answer is going to be "no." If we make a mistake in our job, the expectation is that we will do everything in our power to fix the mistake. If for whatever reason we fail, often it will mean going to our manager and asking for assistance. There are very few cases in which it is acceptable to go back to the customer and ask her to fix the problem.

Why, then, do we build software that expects the caller to deal with the problem? Whether we are throwing exceptions or returning failures, we are putting the responsibility back on the customer rather than keeping it where it belongs—with the software that caused the failure. Granted, there are cases for which we have simply exceeded our ability to fix the problem and we need to go back to the customer. In our restaurant analogy, if the customer ordered something that is no longer available, we will need to go back to the customer and ask her to pick something else. But generally, this type of response should be the last resort. It should be the option we take only when we have exhausted all other attempts to recover from the failure.

Akka is built around the idea that the callers are not responsible for handling failure. It is up to the actor that failed to deal with the problem. And in the event that actor can't handle it, it can ask for help from its "supervisor." This is exactly like our restaurant. And much like our restaurant, we accept that sometimes failures can result in delays, but that doesn't mean that our request won't ever be completed. We are not looking for global temporal consistency. We are embracing the asynchronous, and potentially faulty, nature of the system.

Types of Failures

Before we discuss in detail different ways that we can deal with failure, it is first important to recognize the different types of failures that might occur in our system. Oftentimes when we begin talking about failure and faults we think about exceptions and crashes. Although these are some of the more common errors that might occur, there are other types of failures that we need to think about when developing a reactive system.

Exceptions

Exceptions are one of the most common ways by which a system might fail. When a failure occurs in some code, it will bubble up through the code as an exception that contains a fair amount of useful information about the nature of the exception, including the message and the call stack. This is all important information that you can use to debug the error and trace exactly what happens. A well-designed exception can be a valuable tool in your toolbox when trying to recover from the error.

Exceptions can occur in a number of different situations. You might get exceptions when trying to call code in an external library (e.g., when interoperating with Java). Or one might occur due to a mathematical error. You can also get exceptions when trying to perform illegal operations on certain collection types in Scala (e.g., calling `.get` on `None`). Some of these exceptions are best handled simply by reevaluating your types or your code (e.g., calling `.get` on an `Option` is usually a sign that something is wrong). These are exceptions that occur within your code. But others can occur in situations that are beyond your control. You can't control whether the external library throws an exception. Granted, you could wrap that exception in a Try construct within your own code rather than throwing it, but that doesn't change the fact that you need to deal with the exception at some point.

Fatal Errors in the JVM

There are, of course, other classes of errors. Some errors can't be handled. In the JVM, a fatal error such as an out-of-memory error is going to bring down the system no matter what you do. Catching that error is pointless. In this case, wrapping it in a Try construct isn't going to help; Try constructs don't work with fatal errors, as they only handle nonfatal errors.

Fatal errors are trickier to deal with because they fall outside the normal error handling of the actor system. You can't deal with them by using the normal methods, but that doesn't mean you can ignore them. It just means that you need to be more clever about how you handle them.

External Service Failures

Dealing with external APIs presents its own set of challenges. Usually those APIs are interfaced by using some form of network protocol. The network is never 100 percent reliable. Sometimes you might get connection failures, or failures of other types. In addition, often when you are working with an API, the API might remain responsive and even return results, but sometimes those results include an error code. These things are all beyond your control. There are seldom any options to modify the external API to eliminate the errors, and you definitely don't have the power to prevent all possible network problems. You simply need to deal with these errors. Much like when dealing with an external library, you can choose to wrap the errors in an exception or a Try, but you can't avoid them altogether.

Failing to Meet a Service-Level Agreement

Even if you build a system that is somehow incredibly reliable, there will still be failures that need to be managed. Even if you were able to build a system that never suffered from network issues and had zero conditions in the code that would result in an exception, you can still suffer from failures. Although your system might be guaranteed to always return a result, and for that result to never be an error, there is no guarantee that it will do so in a reasonable amount of time. The best systems can still fall victim to heavy load. And under heavy loads those systems might fail to meet a predefined service-level agreement (SLA). Even though taking 10 seconds to fulfill a user request might technically be successful, from the business perspective, it might represent a total failure. If that request was a simple web page load, there is a good chance your users will have left. These types of failures are interesting because although the software might be doing everything "correctly," it has once again failed to take into account that time is a factor.

Operating System and Hardware-Level Failures

Of course, even if you created a piece of software that always produces a correct result, never had a need to communicate with a network, was totally performant (or perhaps didn't need to be), and never ran out of memory, what happens when the hardware running that application fails? What happens if a hard drive fails, or the operating system of the machine crashes? Again, these are failures that are beyond your control, but you still need to deal with them. Is your user going to accept your explanation that you can't fulfill his request because a hard drive failed? How long are you going to be down while you fix that problem? Can your users simply go to the competition if that happens? How much business will you lose as a result of not properly preparing for this?

Isolating Failures

As we have seen, there are many different types of failures that can occur in a software system with even a small amount of complexity. As the complexity of the system grows, so does the potential complexity of those failures. If you aren't careful about how you build the system, even the most insignificant of errors can bring down the entire system. An uncaught division by zero error could find its way to the top of the system and crash the entire thing. Heavy load on the system could tie up all the threads and grind everything to a halt.

The first key step when dealing with failures in your system, no matter what shape they might take, is to isolate them. You need to build systems wherein a single failure in one area of the system is isolated from other areas so that if that failure does occur, it only affects a small portion of the system rather than the entire thing. Akka provides a few different facilities that help you in this respect.

Bulkheading

One of the simplest ways to isolate failures in Akka is by using a pattern called *bulkheading*. The term bulkheading comes from the nautical world in which ships are built in a series of watertight sections, with each section separated by bulkheads (Figure 7-1). The idea is that if any one section of the ship is breached, the bulkheads would prevent the water from flowing into the other sections. One section of the ship would be lost to water, but other areas would remain safe. This allows the ship to continue to operate after what otherwise might have been a catastrophic failure.

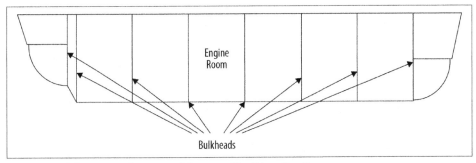

Figure 7-1. The nautical origin of the term "bulkheading"

Akka provides facilities to assist with bulkheading in the form of *actor hierarchies*. A well-designed actor system can use these hierarchies to create isolated failure zones within the application. The idea is that if any portion of the system fails, that failure is isolated to the branch of the tree that contains the failure. Other branches are unaffected and can continue to operate independently from the failure.

Let's consider an example from our sample problem domain. Suppose that you are attempting to fulfill a project request. There are several people who can carry out the specific needs of the project. If we represent each person with an actor, you can send the request to each actor and ask them to evaluate themselves against the required criteria. Because you are using actors, this evaluation can be done concurrently (which is a big advantage), but it also allows you to create failure zones within your application, as illustrated in Figure 7-2. Suppose that you have some bad data in the system. When one of your actors goes to process the request, it encounters this bad data and a failure occurs. If that is the only actor to encounter the bad data, you certainly don't want that failure to affect the other actors. Instead, you can isolate the actor that encountered the failure, leaving the other actors to continue to process the request, and perhaps one of them will be able to meet the required criteria. You should definitely generate an alert of some kind that the bad data was encountered, but there is no need to fail the request completely.

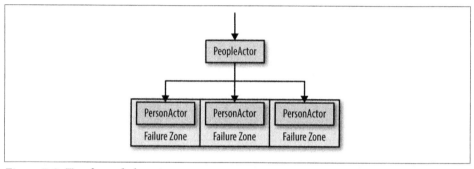

Figure 7-2. Two bounded contexts

Isolating the actor with the failure in this way applies not just in the case of bad data. Whether it's bad data, a failed call to an external API, or even excessive load on that particular actor, all of these cases are effectively isolated to that actor (though in some cases the dispatcher for the actor might also be affected). By creating a strong actor hierarchy you can further isolate your failures. For example, if you were to use a pattern of one actor per request, you can isolate any failures to just that single request. You can break it down even further if required and have an actor to process specific days in the request. This would allow you to isolate failures to just certain periods of time within the request rather than the entire request:

```
object PersonActor {
  case class IsQualified(criteria: Set[Qualification])
  case class Qualified(personId: PersonId)
  case class NotQualified(personId: PersonId)

  def props(personId: PersonId): Props = {
    Props(new PersonActor(personId))
  }
```

```
    }

    class PersonActor(personId: PersonId) extends Actor {
      import PersonActor._

      private def isQualified(criteria: Set[Qualification]): Boolean = ...

      override def receive: Receive = {
        case IsQualified(criteria) =>
          if(isQualified(criteria)) {
            sender ! Qualified(personId)
          } else {
            sender ! NotQualified(personId)
          }
      }
    }

    object PeopleActor {
      case class CreatePerson(id: PersonId)
      case class FindQualifiedPeople(criteria: Set[Qualification])
    }

    class PeopleActor extends Actor {
      import PeopleActor._
      private var people = Map.empty[PersonId, ActorRef]

      protected def createPerson(personId: PersonId) = {
        context.actorOf(PersonActor.props(personId))
      }

      override def receive: Actor.Receive = {
        case CreatePerson(id) =>
          people = people + (id -> createPerson(id))
        case FindQualifiedPeople(criteria) =>
          people.values.foreach {
            person =>
              person.forward(PersonActor.IsQualified(criteria))
          }
      }
    }
```

This example presents a set of `PersonActor`s being managed by a `PeopleActor`. You can ask that `PeopleActor` to find people who have a certain set of qualifications. This is done by forwarding the individual people an `IsQualified` message. The actors can then respond to the original request, indicating whether they are qualified or not. Each `PersonActor` acts as its own failure zone. If one `PersonActor` experiences a failure, it doesn't prevent the others from continuing to perform their work. The exception can be isolated to that individual actor.

Of course, this works only for certain types of failures. Although this type of bulkheading is effective for exceptions, certain SLA failures, and some external API failures, it is not going to be effective in the case of fatal errors, nor is it going to help you handle hardware failures. For those types of failures, you need to use a different approach.

Graceful Degradation

The problem with bulkheading using just an actor hierarchy is that it is still limited to a single machine, and a single Java Virtual Machine (JVM); if the failure occurs at the hardware level and the entire machine goes down, you still lose the entire system. Or, even if there is no hardware failure, if you consume all available resources on the machine, it is still possible to slow the application to the point of being unresponsive when you need it to be. Either way, you are still going to have users complaining because the software isn't working.

To truly protect against failure, you need to be able to isolate even hardware-related problems. But to do that you need to be able to scale beyond a single machine. If your application resides on only one piece of hardware, there is no way to protect against failure of that piece of hardware.

What you need to do in this case is to break the application into smaller pieces and distribute those pieces across multiple machines. In most cases the best way to do this is to revisit the domain-driven design (DDD) concept of a bounded context. Bounded contexts provide natural pieces of a system that you can separate into discrete units. The nature of a bounded context means that it will have very few resources that it shares with other parts of the system. This makes it easier to split it into a separate subsystem. That subsystem can then be moved over to another piece of hardware. This in turn creates a new failure zone.

Well, yes, technically. But by splitting your bounded contexts across multiple machines, you provision against the failure of that hardware. This way, if one piece of hardware fails, you will lose a piece of the application, but hopefully not the entire system. Other aspects of the system that don't rely on the failed piece can continue to operate despite the faulty hardware.

Let's look at another example. Figure 7-3 shows that our sample system has a bounded context for creating people and recording information about the skills those people possess. This context is called the Skills Matrix. There is also a separate context, the Proposal Service, that will run a proposal against the people defined in the Skills Matrix to generate a proposal based on the people's skills. If these were all running on a single piece of hardware in a single JVM, a failure could bring down the entire system. But by separating these bounded contexts and running them on different hardware, you protect against failures to some extent. Now suppose that the Proposal Service were to encounter a fatal hardware-related error. As a result, you lose the ability to generate new proposals. But you can still create new people and assign skills to those people because that aspect of the system is running on a separate piece of hardware.

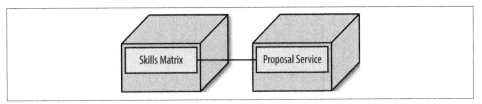

Figure 7-3. Remote failure zones

On the flip side, if it were the hardware running the Skills Matrix that you lost, but the Proposal Service remained active, the nature of the problem changes. Depending on how you design the Proposal Service, it might have a dependency on the Skills Matrix. If this is the case, when you lose the Skills Matrix, you might lose portions of the Proposal Service, as well. It will no longer be able to look up people and their skills. But that doesn't mean you must lose the entire thing. You might still be able to view previous proposal results because those have already been computed. You might be able to perform limited actions on those proposals as long as those actions don't require a lookup to the Skills Matrix. The point here is that even though the loss of the Skills Matrix has an effect on the functionality of the Proposal Service, it doesn't automatically mean it's a crippling problem.

This type of bulkheading is something we see quite often in our day-to-day use of software. Have you ever gone to a website and noticed that a small portion of that site is unavailable? Most of the website might be functional, but a piece of it has been disabled or has failed. You might try to perform an action on the site only to get a message like, "Sorry, this feature is currently unavailable." This is called *graceful degradation*. The idea is that rather than the entire site failing, only portions of it fail, leaving some features unavailable while other features remain active.

Of course, bulkheading in this manner is not specific to Akka. This is something that represents a good practice no matter what tool you are using to build your application. So how does Akka fit into this specifically?

First, let's go back to the idea of global temporal consistency. If we eliminate the need for global temporal consistency, we open up new possibilities. If we send a request to an application that it cannot immediately fulfill, the normal pattern is to fail. But, if we embrace the asynchronous reality that we live in, perhaps a failure is not required. Perhaps, instead of, "Sorry, this feature is currently unavailable," we could return a message like, "Your request has been accepted and you will be notified when it is complete." Just because an area of the system has failed doesn't mean we can't still accept the request. We just need to wait until the system is fully operational again before we can process that message. In some cases, it might not even require a message. If we ask Facebook to send a friend request, does it matter if it completes that now or sometime in the next three hours? Not really. Does the user need any feedback if that request takes longer than expected? Probably not. When we accept that the world operates in an asynchronous manner, we can begin to build our systems to support that. Systems built in this way become naturally more amenable to the types of separation that enable bulkheading.

Isolating Failure by Using Akka Cluster

Bulkheading is a useful technique and there are many ways in which you can achieve it, regardless of whether you are using Akka. The benefit with Akka is that it has built-in support for features that enable bulkheading and make its usage more transparent. Akka Cluster and its related extensions provide a variety of features that make isolating failures easier.

With Akka Cluster, you can communicate with actors on remote JVMs transparently. Although the method of instantiating the actor might be slightly different for a clustered actor, the actual communication mechanism doesn't change. This means that when you make the decision to move an actor to a cluster, you don't need to change anything about the communication protocol. This makes it fairly trivial to split up systems of actors after the fact. You can move those actors to different JVMs or different machines with a minimal amount of code changed.

Of course, doing this arbitrarily is probably not a good idea. Instead, there are particular patterns that you should follow when using Akka Cluster to isolate failure. If you have sections of your actor hierarchy that represent a bounded context, those become obvious choices to split out using Akka Cluster.

You also can use tools like Akka cluster sharding to split collections of actors among multiple machines. Using cluster sharding, you can take a set of actors and partition it into multiple subsets. These subsets can then reside on different machines. For example, you could shard your Person actors. The benefit here is that if a failure occurs on any of the "shards," only a subset of the Person actors will be affected, leaving many of your actors able to continue to operate, unaffected by the failure. An added benefit of cluster sharding is that it can automatically redistribute failed actors to other nodes. So if you lose one of your shards, the actors can be re-created somewhere else in the cluster. Of course, any work that was currently in progress on the failed node will be lost unless you have some method of recovering that work, but at least the failure of the actor will be temporary.

Controlling Failures by Using Circuit Breakers

Suppose that the system encountered a failure that caused it to no longer meet your SLA. Calls to a particular piece of the system are timing out. You used bulkheading in some manner to isolate that failure so that the rest of the system can continue to operate. Perhaps the reason for the failure is heavy load on that particular area of the system.

Let's consider what happens if another call comes in to the failed area of the system. That call will be added to the queue for the failing system, and the failing system will need to process it when it can. But that system is already struggling to keep up, which means that the added request is just going to make things worse. As more requests continue to be sent to the failing system, the problem intensifies. Requests take longer and longer without giving the system any time to catch up. Meanwhile, all those requests have an SLA that isn't being met, which means they are timing out. The system might even retry the request, hoping that a second attempt will be successful, but that in turn further compounds the existing problem. This can end up being a big mess.

Let's look at how Akka helps to improve this scenario. Akka provides a tool called a Circuit Breaker that is similar in concept to an electrical circuit breaker in your home. The purpose of an electrical circuit breaker is to detect a fault in the electrical system and shut off the flow of electricity, preventing the problem from becoming worse. An Akka Circuit Breaker serves the same purpose. It is there to detect a fault and shut off the flow of messages in order to prevent the problem from escalating.

An Akka Circuit Breaker is used to wrap what might be considered a "dangerous" call. The dangerous call can be either a synchronous call that returns a value or throws an exception, or it could be an asynchronous call that returns a future. During normal operation the calls will be handled as expected. Each successful execution resets a failure counter to zero. In this case, the breaker is in the "closed" state.

When the dangerous call wrapped by the Circuit Breaker begins to fail, the behavior of the breaker changes. The failure counter begins to increment with each failure until it reaches a configurable maximum. When this maximum value is reached, the breaker moves into the "open" state. In the open state, the breaker automatically fails all calls. This means that it won't even attempt the calls. Instead, it just automatically generates a failure; in this case, the failure is a CircuitBreakerOpenException. These failures happen quickly because there is no need to even attempt to do the call. The Circuit Breaker will continue to operate in the open state for a configurable time period.

After the configured time period has elapsed, the Circuit Breaker will move into a "half-open" state. While in the half-open state, the first call coming into the Circuit Breaker will be allowed to proceed as though it were in the closed state. If this call succeeds, the breaker will move into the closed state and normal operation can resume. If the first call fails, though, the breaker will move back into the open state and it will continue to automatically fail the calls. If it does move back to the open state, it will again stay in that state for the configured time period (Figure 7-4).

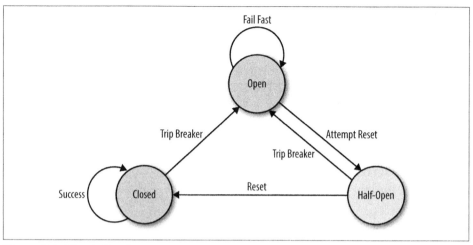

Figure 7-4. Circuit Breaker states

The benefit to using the Circuit Breaker is that it provides a way for you to give the failing system time to recover. Rather than continuing to call it, potentially making the problem worse, you instead automatically fail the calls without even trying the failed system. You should do this for a period of time, during which the failed system has an opportunity to recover. If it recovers and you make another call, it will succeed and normal operation will continue. If the system does not recover by the end of the time period, you will let through only a single call before automatically failing. In this way, you have created only a small amount of load on that failed system and avoided overstressing it, which will hopefully give the system time to recover.

Creating an Akka Circuit Breaker is fairly simple:

```
val circuitBreaker = new CircuitBreaker(
  context.system.scheduler,
  maxFailures = 5,
  callTimeout = 5.seconds,
  resetTimeout = 30.seconds)
```

This creates a Circuit Breaker that will allow for a maximum of five failures. It also includes a `callTimeout` so that if the call doesn't fail but simply takes too long to complete, that too can be counted as a failure. Finally, there is a `resetTimeout`. This sets the length of time that the system must wait after the breaker is in the open state before it can transition to the half-open state.

You can use the Circuit Breaker to wrap both synchronous and asynchronous calls. For an asynchronous call, you can do something like the following:

```
val result = circuitBreaker.withCircuitBreaker {
  (people ? CreatePerson(id)).mapTo[PersonCreated]
}
```

The call to `withCircuitBreaker` wraps the future passed into it such that the result will still be a future of the same type containing the result if the call succeeds, or the resulting exception if the call fails. But if the Circuit Breaker is in an open state, that future will instead fail with a `CircuitBreakerOpenException`.

To wrap a synchronous call, do the following:

```
val result = circuitBreaker.withSyncCircuitBreaker {
  // dangerous code
}
```

This returns the result of the call directly without wrapping it in a future. It is a blocking call. If the Circuit Breaker is open, the call to `withSyncCircuitBreaker` will throw the `CircuitBreakerOpenException`.

Dealing with Failures

Although isolating and controlling failures is important for building a strong system, it isn't enough by itself. You can use techniques like graceful degradation and circuit breakers to keep the problem from spreading, but what happens if you need to recover from the problem? Or, can you simply prevent the problem from even occurring in the first place?

Let's return to our restaurant example. Our customer has placed her order. During the preparation of the order, the plate was dropped. We successfully isolate this problem by having the dropped order affect only the cook. The servers can still continue to take additional orders and carry out other assigned tasks. Hosts can seat new guests. Existing guests can leave, and their tables are cleared and prepared for the next customers. In other words, the business does not need to come to a complete halt because of one problem that affects one order. But what about the kitchen? Assume for a moment that our restaurant has just a single cook. That cook has dropped the order and now something must be done about it. Just isolating the problem isn't enough. At some point, the cook is going to have to remake the order, or the customer is going to be very unhappy. He can't just move on to the next order. Granted there are other people waiting for their food, too, but that doesn't mean we give up on the dropped order. In addition to isolating the problem, we also need to recover from it. So what do we do? Obviously, in the restaurant scenario, we remake the order. If the time to remake the order is small, we can do so without even informing anyone; there is no need to trouble everyone else with the details. If it will take some time to re-create, we might want to inform the server who might need to inform the customer. But only if necessary.

Think about what happened here. The order was dropped. The food was spoiled. Did we try to prevent that problem from happening? There are likely policies and procedures governing our restaurant's operation that assist with preventing these kinds of problems, but we accept that those procedures will not be perfect. We accept that no matter how careful our cooks are, at some point a meal will be dropped. This is just a fact of life in a busy restaurant. So rather than trying to prevent every dropped order, we instead implement policies and procedures to deal with those situations when they occur.

It's the same with Akka. We do our best to prevent failures, but we recognize that they are a reality. When they happen we simply "let it crash." It's how we recover from that crash that makes our system resilient. Understanding the "let it crash" mentality is critical to building reactive systems. All systems, no matter the level of complexity, have the potential for failures. If we don't plan for those failures and react accordingly, the system will fail.

The techniques we use to deal with a failure can vary depending on the nature of the failure. We deal with an exception differently than we deal with a hardware failure. And yet, at the core, we can apply the mentality of "let it crash" no matter at what level the failure occurs.

Dealing with Exceptions (Let It Crash)

Another form of failure is when the code itself throws an exception. Here we'll explore techniques for dealing with this problem.

Nonfatal exceptions

Within an application, the primary form of failure with which you need to be concerned is exceptions. More specifically, you need to be concerned with nonfatal exceptions. These are the exceptions that don't necessarily bring down the entire system. We can recover from these failures within the scope of the application. So how do you do that?

Within a single actor, you can try to deal with failures where you know they might occur. If you expect a method could throw an exception, wrap that method in a try–catch block and then handle the exception when it occurs. This will keep the errors isolated within that actor. But this doesn't always work. Sometimes, the nature of the error is such that the actor in which the exception occurs is not capable of dealing with the problem.

Thinking about our restaurant example, if the cook drops the meal, he can just remake it. But what happens if he has run out of ingredients? Now he might not be able to handle the problem on his own and might need to involve other people. The cook might need to go to the restaurant manager to determine the best course of action.

In Akka, when an exception is not handled by the actor, the actor's supervisor is alerted that there has been an exception. It is then up to the supervisor to decide how to handle the exception. This is done through a *supervisor strategy*. Every actor has the potential to create children and therefore be a supervisor. For this reason every actor also has a supervisor strategy. A default strategy is applied if no specific strategy has been defined.

There are two types of `supervisorStrategy` built in to Akka: `OneForOneStrategy` and `AllForOneStrategy`. The `OneForOneStrategy` directs the supervisor to apply the recovery logic to only the failing actor. Other actors remain unaffected. Conversely, the `AllForOneStrategy` signals the supervisor to instead apply the recovery logic to all of its children.

Let's consider our scheduling domain example. Suppose that we are attempting to schedule a project. We have defined that project and then sent off the request to multiple Person actors to see if any of them can fulfill the needs of the project. If one of those actors fails on a database lookup, it might not be necessary to affect all the Person actors. We might need only affect the actor that failed. This would be a good use case for the `OneForOneStrategy`. On the other hand, what if it turned out that the incoming project data was invalid in some way. In this case, any actor attempting to process that data is likely going to fail for the same reason. In this case, there is no point in waiting for all of the actors to fail. We already know that will happen. This would be a good use case for the `AllForOneStrategy`. The logic here can be applied to all the child actors.

A `supervisorStrategy` also includes a `Decider`. A `Decider` is a `PartialFunction[Throwable, Directive]`. The `Decider` has the job of determining what course of action to take depending on what type of Exception has occurred. A `Decider` basically maps from the exception type to one of the following directives:

Resume

> The `Resume` directive tells the supervisor that the failing actor should continue processing messages as though no failure occurred. No change in state occurs. This is useful if the actor is stateless or if the actor's state has not been invalidated by the failure.

Restart

> The `Restart` directive tells the supervisor that the failing actor should be restarted. This means that the existing actor will be stopped and a new actor will be put in its place. This will result in any state for that actor being reset to the initial state. This is useful if the actor's state has been invalidated by the failure.

Stop

> The `Stop` directive tells the supervisor that the failing actor should be stopped and not replaced. This directive is useful if the failure results in an actor that is no longer needed or that can't be recovered in any way. For example, if it was a

single-use actor, created only to accomplish the current task, and that task fails, the actor is no longer needed and we can just stop it.

Escalate

If the supervisor is unable to provide an appropriate action to take for the given failure, we can escalate that failure. This essentially results in the supervisor failing, and it will be up to its supervisor to handle the failure, instead. Think of this like rethrowing an exception.

We can now create a `supervisorStrategy` for one of the People actors. The People actor has the responsibility of supervising the Person actors. A very simple strategy for this People actor might look like this:

```
override val supervisorStrategy =
  OneForOneStrategy() {
    case _: AskTimeoutException => Resume
    case _: IllegalArgumentException => Stop
  }
```

This is a very trivial example. In this case, if you get an `AskTimeoutException`, you are assuming that the state of the actor is not corrupted. Maybe you can try the `Ask` again or move onto the next message, so we will simply resume when that occurs. For the `IllegalArgumentException`, let's assume that this occurs due to a problem with the data being passed into the constructor of the actor. If that data is illegal in some way, resuming or restarting the actor isn't going to help. Instead, you should stop the actor.

But simply providing a trivial action like this usually isn't enough. Presumably, you want this actor to do something. So, when it fails, you probably don't want to just ignore the failure. You probably also want to take some additional recovery actions. You might want to resend the failed message to try again. Perhaps you want to redirect that failed message to another actor to see if that actor can complete the task instead. Or, you might want to perform any number of other complex activities in order to properly recover from the failure.

In our restaurant, it isn't sufficient for the manager to tell the cook to just keep going about his business. The lost order needs to be remade—or if it can't be, something else needs to be done to recover from the situation. The server might need to go back to the customer to explain the situation. These actions all need to be initiated, probably by the manager.

A supervisor strategy doesn't need to be a simple mapping from an exception to a directive. You can put additional logic in, as well. For example, when you receive a particular exception, you could send a message to an actor to deal with that exception. You also could change the state of the supervisor if necessary. These options open up interesting possibilities for recovering from a failure. As long as you include enough information in the exception, it becomes possible for the supervisor to perform any steps necessary to recover from the error.

Let's take a very simple example. If a message fails to be processed for some reason, you might include that message within the exception:

```
case class MessageException(msg: Message, cause: Throwable) extends
  Exception(s"The Message Failed to Process: $msg", cause)
```

When that message is available, you can make use of it within the supervisor Strategy:

```
override val supervisorStrategy =
  OneForOneStrategy() {
    case MessageException(msg) =>
      sender ! msg
      Resume
  }
```

This is a very simple example of a self-healing system. In this case, when the exception occurs, you wrap it inside another exception and include the message in that exception. This gives the supervisor access to that message. The supervisor receives the exception, extracts the message, resends the message to the actor, and then directs the actor to resume processing. In this way, you essentially get to retry the failed message.

In truth, this isn't a great way to solve this particular problem. We use it here as a simple demonstration that you can do more than simply return a directive. A much better solution would be to leverage the AtLeastOnceDelivery mechanism covered in Chapter 6. This is far more customizable and allows the retry to be persistent as well.

The logic here can be as simple or as complex as it needs to be. In a more complicated situation, you might decide to not send the message back to the same actor. You might conclude that because that actor has failed, it is no longer useful. Instead, you might decide to send the message to a different child actor, or spawn a new actor for the sole purpose of handling the exception. Or, you might add the message to some kind of error queue and deal with it later. The key is that you recognize that the failure has occurred and take appropriate steps to recover from it. You want to build the system in such a way that it is self healing.

Of course, all of this leads to an obvious question: aren't we still just dealing with known exceptions? What happens if an unexpected error occurs? For unexpected exceptions, the obvious approach is to put a case in the Decider to handle generic nonfatal exceptions. You can then decide what to do with that exception. On first glance, that might seem unintuitive. How can we deal with an exception properly if we don't know what that exception will be ahead of time? In a well-designed actor with a very specific use case and small message protocol, this should actually be relatively easy. A well-designed actor will have only a few possible recovery strategies.

You then just need to pick from that very limited set of strategies to determine how to behave if something unexpected occurs. If you find yourself in a situation in which there seems to be too many strategies to pick from and none of them stand out as the obvious choice, you have probably made the actor too large and need to look at decomposing it. On the other hand, if the actor is fairly simple but you still have cases for which you aren't sure how to react to an unexpected error, you might be looking at the wrong level of the hierarchy. You might need to either move down to one of the children to handle the unexpected cases or escalate the exception.

Fatal errors in the JVM

Sometimes, no matter how careful you are, an error occurs that you can't handle. In these cases, whether it is an out-of-memory error, or a stack overflow, or some other error, the system is going to terminate. In these cases, there is little that you can do to heal the error within the JVM. The system crashes, and you are done.

Does this mean that you should accept these types of crashes as a fact of life and require manual intervention to recover? Or are there tools that you can use to recover even in the event of a catastrophic failure of this kind? Even for failures that are going to bring down the system, you can take steps when designing the system that will help it to recover from even the worst kinds of failures.

The first thing you need in order to provide self healing in the case of an absolute failure of the system is some way for the failed application to be restarted. There is nothing specific to Akka by which you can do this, but there are tools available that can help. Lightbend offers its own solution for this: ConductR. ConductR is a tool that you can use to create a cluster and specify how many of each application you want running. In the event that an application fails, ConductR will ensure that a new instance of that application is launched somewhere in the cluster to compensate. Other orchestration tools such as Mesos and Docker Swarm also provide solutions for ensuring that instances of an application remain running.

Whether you use ConductR or an alternative application, the basic idea is the same. You need to have an application that will monitor your process in some way. If that process fails, the monitoring application will automatically restart it. This is a bit like your Akka supervisors, only in this case the directive is always `Restart`, and rather than detecting exceptions, you are determining failure by using other means.

Monitoring your applications and automatically restarting them can be a lifesaver from an operations perspective. We have seen cases in which an application has a severe bug that causes it to restart every couple of minutes, yet despite this, the application has been able to serve clients all night simply because every time it failed the monitoring application restarted it. And due to the asynchronous reactive design of the system, clients were unaware that a problem had occurred. This type of setup can save you from the dreaded 3 A.M. phone call.

But it's not enough just to restart the application. This is a step in the right direction, but much like with our nonfatal errors, we also need to have some kind of self-healing mechanism in place to recover from the failure. So how can you implement self healing in a system like this?

The key to healing these systems is to have a fallback point in the application. You need a point in the system at which you can draw a line in the sand and say that when the system reaches that point, your data is safe. Prior to that point, any failures will result in the loss of that data; after that point, any failures will be recoverable using the data that was provided up to that point. The ideal circumstance is to push that point as close to the beginning of the process as possible. You want to reach your safe point as quickly as possible. What does that look like in a real system?

Let's look at our scheduling domain example. Upon making a request to the scheduling domain to perform the scheduling actions for a particular project, when do we consider that command to be complete? Do we consider it complete when the project has been fully scheduled and all the results are known? That is the end goal, but what if that takes hours? We don't really want to have any processes that take hours, so how can we simplify that?

A better way to handle this is to consider the command to be done as soon as it is accepted and persisted. In other words, when we make a request to schedule a project, we take that request, push it on to a persistent queue of some kind, and then at that point, we can send an acknowledgment back to the client saying that its command has been accepted and will be processed asynchronously. A failure before the command is persisted will result in an error to the client. A failure after the command has been persisted will result in a retry or engaging some kind of self-healing logic.

There are many ways that you might implement this kind of logic, but they all rely on one simple concept: all of them require At Least Once delivery. You need to be able to guarantee that a message will be delivered, even if a failure occurs. One way to do this is to use an external persistent message bus. You want a message bus that will deliver to a client and allow the client to acknowledge receipt of the message. If you have this, you can use it to provide us with automatic retries. When a command enters the system, it performs any validation required on that command and then converts it to another message. That message is then sent to the message bus. After the message is sent to the message bus, the command is considered complete. After that point, any further processing happens asynchronously and failure is no longer an option. You might delay processing due to an error, but that processing will eventually be recovered. If the message is unable to be delivered or is not acknowledged, the message bus will retry at a later point.

Within the context of Akka, you can use tools like Akka Persistence to achieve a similar effect. Again there are multiple ways by which you can do this, but let's look at one possibility. Akka Persistence introduces the concept of At Least Once delivery. You can take advantage of this to provide a message delivery guarantee. The Command processor can receive the command, validate it, and then send the resulting message into the system by using `AtLeastOnceDelivery`. This means that if the system fails to receive and acknowledge the message, the Command processor will resend it. It will continue to resend until you have confirmation that the message has been completed. This gives you a form of reliable delivery, but it also provides the retry mechanism you were looking for. You can now guarantee that the message will eventually be handled. Even if the Command processor were to fail, because it is a persistent actor, when it is re-created it will continue to try to send that message.

Here's your fallback point in the event of an error. If an error occurs in the system and you are unable to finish processing the message, the message will not be acknowledged. This will then force the system to retry the message at a later date. Depending on the complexity of the message, it might be necessary to create multiple fallback points within the message processing pipeline. Throughout the pipeline, you can use `PersistentActors` and `AtLeastOnceDelivery` where required to ensure that if the system experiences a catastrophic failure, it can re-create the necessary state for it to continue.

This only works in a system that has embraced an asynchronous design. If your system is trapped by the need to make everything synchronous, you lose this capability. In a synchronous system, you can't allow failure. Everything needs to complete successfully before the system acknowledges that the command has been completed. If a piece of the system fails, you need to fail the command. You can't wait 15 minutes for that piece of the system to be reestablished. On the other hand, if the system is mostly asynchronous, this isn't a problem. The system can accept the command and persist it. If it can't be completed now, perhaps due to a failure in the system, the system can try to complete it later, after it comes back online. No one needs to even know that the failure occurred.

Dealing with External Service Failures

Most systems will eventually encounter a situation in which they need to communicate with an external service. That external service is completely beyond our control. There is nothing we can do to that service to improve its resiliency. And sometimes that service will fail. So how can we deal with those failures?

Dealing with external service failures actually ends up being a combination of the techniques we used to deal with internal failures. The first thing we need to do is to isolate the failures so that we can degrade gracefully. The techniques for isolating those failures are no different than if we were dealing with internal systems. We can treat the external system as another bounded context. We create a wrapper around that external system. If the external system fails, our ability to execute certain operations will be hindered, but we keep the rest of the system running so that commands that don't require the external system can continue to operate.

We can also use persistent queues and other techniques so that while the external system is down we can buffer messages. When the system comes back up, we can replay the messages from the persistent queue. This could be as simple as using `AtLeast OnceDelivery` to a wrapper actor around the external service.

Let's look at a simple example of what this might look like:

```scala
object ProjectAPIActor {

  case class CreateProject(projectId: ProjectId)
  case class ProjectCreatedSent(projectId: ProjectId)

  def props(remotePath: ActorPath): Props =
    Props(new ProjectAPIActor(remotePath))
}

class ProjectAPIActor(remotePath: ActorPath)
  extends PersistentActor
  with AtLeastOnceDelivery {
  import ProjectAPIActor._

  override val persistenceId: String = self.path.name

  private val projectActor = createProjectActor()
  protected def createProjectActor() = {
    context.actorSelection(remotePath)
  }

  private def handleSend(msg: ProjectCreatedSent) = {
    deliver(projectActor) {
      deliveryId =>
        ProjectActor.CreateProject(deliveryId, msg.projectId)
    }
  }

  private def handleConfirm(confirm: ProjectActor.ProjectCreated): Unit = {
    confirmDelivery(confirm.deliveryId)
  }

  override def receiveRecover: Receive = {
    case ProjectCreatedSent(projectId) =>
      handleSend(ProjectCreatedSent(projectId))
    case confirm: ProjectActor.ProjectCreated =>
      handleConfirm(confirm)
  }

  override def receiveCommand: Receive = {
    case CreateProject(projectId) =>
      persist(ProjectCreatedSent(projectId))(handleSend)
```

```
      case confirm: ProjectActor.ProjectCreated =>
        persist(confirm)(handleConfirm)
  }
}
```

This code presents a ProjectAPI that talks to a ProjectActor. The ProjectActor is remote and might fail for any number of reasons. It is worth noting, however, that this technique could still be applied whether ProjectActor was local or remote.

The remote ProjectActor will be responsible for handling the command. Assuming that the call is successful, it sends a response back to the sender. This is simple enough. The only interesting thing here is that in the message protocol we have included the deliveryId, which is an ID provided by the AtLeastOnceDelivery trait.

In the API, when you send a message, you now use the AtLeastOnceDelivery mechanism. Here, you use the deliver method rather than our usual tell or ask. This is combined with the persist call so that if a failure occurs, the system can try to redeliver. It also then looks for the response, and when it receives it, it can confirmDelivery by using the deliveryId. Using this combination of deliver and confirmDelivery, you can provide the kind of guarantee you need. If the external service were to fail, the message would not be confirmed. The message would then be redelivered later after a configurable delay.

You can use AtLeastOnceDelivery in multiple places in the pipeline if necessary. This example demonstrates it only around the external service, but there is no reason why you can't use it in other places. Be careful, though: overusing AtLeastOnceDelivery might suggest that you are still trying to achieve global consistency. AtLeastOnce Delivery is probably best used at either end of a pipeline of calls. You probably don't want to use it at every stage of the pipeline.

Conclusion

Now that you have seen how actor-based systems treat failure as an expected situation and integrate their reaction to failures at every level into normal operations, you can see how actor-based distributed systems are far less likely to suffer *systems*-level failures, and far more likely to recover from the partial failures they do encounter than other approaches.

This helps reduce downtime in your system. But the reality is that while you have provided ways to isolate and recover from failure, the failure still exists. What you need now is a way to increase redundancy in the system so that when a failure occurs, you can have something to fall back on. In Chapter 8, we will discuss in depth some of the techniques you can use to increase availability in your system, even in the face of failure.

Availability

One of the key requirements in reactive programming is that your system must provide *availability*. But what does it mean for a system to be available? We can consider a system available when it is able to respond to requests in a timely manner. If the system takes too long to respond, or in fact doesn't respond at all, it is considered unavailable. A system is unavailable when it is down or overloaded.

Availability is distinct from the ability of the system to scale (e.g., *scalability*).

As detailed in Chapter 7, there are many things that can contribute to the system becoming unavailable. And no matter how much we try, there will be times when pieces of the system will become unavailable. The key, then, is to find ways to mitigate that, so that even in the face of failures, the system can remain available. We have already discussed how you can address specific types of failures. This chapter provides a higher-level look at how you can build systems in a way that supports availability, and what features Akka provides to get you there.

Microservices Versus Monoliths

Today, there are two often-discussed approaches to building applications. Applications can either be *monolithic* or they can be built using *microservices*. Both approaches exist on either end of a spectrum on which most software projects fall somewhere in between. Very few applications are completely monolithic or perfect microservices.

Monolithic applications are built such that all of the components of the application are deployed as a single unit. Complexity in monolithic applications is isolated by creating libraries that are then knitted together into the larger whole.

Microservices, on the other hand, are built by dividing the larger application into smaller, specialized services. These microservices perform very small tasks in an isolated fashion. Complexity is isolated to the individual microservices and then put together using other microservices.

Availability is not really a question of monoliths or microservices. You can create highly available applications using either approach. However, the manner in which you do that, and the effects on the scalability of your application, are dependent on which route you choose.

In a monolithic application there is only a single deployable unit. In this case, the way we provide availability—and scalability—is to simply deploy more units. If any one unit is lost, others will pick up the slack. Akka doesn't really help us here. The deployed units don't need to communicate with one another, so there is no need to introduce features like Akka Cluster. Within the monolith, we can use Akka to help us make better use of resources. We can also use it to help isolate faults by using bulkheading and other techniques. Akka does have a place within a monolithic system, but when we are speaking of availability using Akka, we are more interested in techniques that don't fit well in a monolithic application.

Providing availability with microservices is similar to monoliths in that the way to provide it is by deploying multiple instances of each microservice. However, in this case, because each microservice is separate, it can be deployed independently, scaled independently, and our availability needs can be tuned independently. Some areas of a system might be critical and need to be highly available. Other areas might be less important, perhaps only needing to run for a few hours a day or even less. In these cases, availability might be much less of a concern.

When we have multiple microservices that need to communicate with one another, Akka provides facilities that can help. But, before we go into detail about what facilities Akka provides, let's first take a moment to talk about how we divide up an application into microservices.

Bounded Contexts as Microservices

Domain-driven design (DDD) gives us a very natural way to divide an application into smaller pieces. Bounded contexts are excellent boundaries on which to divide. By definition, bounded contexts isolate areas of the domain from one another. Therefore, following this idea, we can isolate areas of our application along the same dividing lines. This means separating those areas out into separate microservices.

Sometimes, those microservices might have some shared elements, and you might need some common libraries in certain cases to share code. In DDD, bounded contexts can share domain elements through what is known as a *shared kernel*. This shared kernel is basically a set of common domain elements that can be used by multiple bounded contexts. In Akka, the message protocol that is passed between clustered applications is commonly found in the shared kernel.

This message protocol, as defined in the shared kernel, represents the API for the bounded context or microservice. It defines the inputs and outputs for that microservice. Depending on the mechanism of communication being used between the microservices, it might consist of a series of simple case classes that are directly sent to other actors, or it might represent case classes that are first serialized to JSON or some other format and then sent via an HTTP call to an Akka HTTP endpoint.

In our scheduling domain example, we have three bounded contexts defined: the User Management context, the Scheduling context, and the Skills context. We can separate each of these into microservices. We can then define either an HTTP endpoint to interact with those services, or we can directly send messages to the actors using Akka Cluster or Akka Remoting.

After we have successfully partitioned our application into microservices, we can then begin thinking about how we want to scale and deploy the application. Certain microservices might need many copies in order to provide scalability, whereas others might, by necessity, be limited to a single copy. Depending on the criteria, this can have an effect on how we make our application available.

Fine-Grained Microservices

Although bounded contexts are a good starting point for dividing up an application, sometimes that's not enough. Sometimes, we need to break things into chunks smaller than a bounded context. A common pattern in Akka is to separate the interface and the domain into separate microservices. In the case of a REST API, that might mean that the REST API exists as a single microservice, whereas the actual logic behind that API could be another. This is advantageous because it makes it possible to scale the two sides independently.

The benefit of Akka is that you can make those types of decisions without affecting the architecture of the application. Location transparency means that we can decide whether we want our REST API in the same deployable unit, or in a separate deployable unit without affecting the basic structure of the application.

In the following section, we will explore several techniques that you can use to break apart an application, all toward the goal of providing the availability and scalability that you want. Which technique is best suited for you depends on the specifics of your system's design.

Cluster-Aware Routers

When building using a single, local actor system, routers are a scalability feature. With them, you can process more messages in parallel which makes it possible to scale up an application within a single machine. However, when dealing with a distributed system, you can also use routers as an availability feature. Cluster-aware routers are like normal routers, except that their routees might reside on other nodes in the cluster. This allows those routers to provide availability on top of scalability.

With a cluster-aware router, you can spin up multiple nodes in your cluster. These nodes can act as hosts to the routees of the router. Then, within your application, when you want to send a message to the actors, you can send it through the cluster-aware router. The router will then ensure that one of the nodes will receive the message, depending on which routing strategy you adopted.

If a node fails, the router can simply direct the message to a different, active node. From the client perspective, you don't need to worry about which node receives the message; the router takes care of that detail for you. But you now have the benefit of added availability, given that nodes can leave the cluster without the client even realizing it. In fact, if you are using a pool router, when a node does leave the cluster, the pool router can even create new routees on other nodes in the cluster in order to compensate for the loss of that node.

One thing to be aware of is that the routing strategies work differently when using cluster-aware routers than they do with local routers. For example, with a smallest-mailbox router, no information is passed between nodes regarding the mailbox size. This means that the smallest mailbox router has no idea which node in the cluster has a smaller mailbox. In this case, the router uses the normal smallest-mailbox logic for all local routees, but remote routees are given lower priority.

So where might you use a cluster-aware router? Cluster-aware routers are a much more general-purpose construct than a cluster singleton, so their use cases are more varied. But a good example of where you might use this is in a worker pattern. In this case, you have a single actor that will push tasks to multiple workers. In our sample domain, for example, we might use the worker pattern to make schedule adjustments. We want to be able to do several schedule adjustments in parallel, particularly because the amount of work involved might be significant. In this case, we can push a message into a router, which will then distribute it to an available worker. Those workers can reside on any node in the cluster. If a node is lost, the workers are lost as well, but depending on the router configuration, they might be reallocated to another node in the cluster.

In practice, this worker pattern might look something like the following:

```scala
object Scheduler {
  case class ScheduleProject(project: Project)
  case class ProjectScheduled(project: Project)

  def props() = Props(new Scheduler)
}

class Scheduler extends Actor {
  import Scheduler._

  override def receive: Receive = {
    case ScheduleProject(project) =>
      // Do Work
      sender() ! ProjectScheduled(project)
  }
}
```

Again, as with the cluster singleton, there is no evidence here that we are going to use Akka Cluster. We can decide that later.

Indeed, creating instances of the workers is no different than creating instances of local actors:

```scala
val scheduler = system.actorOf(Scheduler.props(), "scheduler")
```

This example creates an instance of the actor and names it scheduler. Within your local system, you can treat this just as you would any other actor, because, in fact, it is just a standard actor. The magic happens on another clustered node when you want to refer to this actor:

```scala
val scheduler = system.actorOf(
    ClusterRouterGroup(RoundRobinGroup(Nil), ClusterRouterGroupSettings(
      totalInstances = 100,
      routeesPaths = immutable.Seq("/user/scheduler"),
      allowLocalRoutees = false,
      useRole = None
    )).props(),
    "scheduler"
  )
```

This code configures a cluster-aware group router that references the scheduler. You can see that it has a path to the scheduler, which matches the path that we created for the instance of the actor to which we want to route. In this case, we are allowing up to 100 instances to be used by this group router, but we have only created a single instance. If we had 100 nodes, though, each node could be creating and managing an instance of the scheduler. We could also specify a different sequence of paths for the routee's paths in case the pattern changes from node to node.

This router will now do a lookup on the cluster nodes to find any instances of the scheduler. It will then route messages to those instances—in this case, using a round-robin routing strategy. One thing to note, however, is that unlike the singleton proxy, the router does not buffer messages until a node can be found. This means that if you try to send a message before your node has connected to the cluster and found the routees, that message will be lost. You can help mitigate this by listening to cluster events and only starting to send messages after your cluster is fully established. Of course, Akka's delivery guarantee is still only At Most Once, so if you really need reliable delivery, you will need to use one of the other techniques to achieve that.

Distributed Data

Within an eventually consistent, distributed system, such as the one we are building, we sometimes encounter situations in which there is transient data. This data is not something that needs to be saved in a database. It exists only for the life of the application. If the application is terminated, it is safe to terminate that data, as well. This could include things like user session information. When a user logs in, you might need to store information about that user. When did she log in? What security token did she use? What was the last activity she performed? Information like that is interesting, but keeping it isn't always valuable. After the user has logged out, that information becomes irrelevant and potentially needs to be cleaned up.

At the same time, it might be important that the transient information be available on all nodes. If a user is experiencing network problems and she becomes disconnected and then reconnected, she might end up reconnected to a different node. If that information is unavailable, the system loses its value. What this situation calls for is a way to maintain this data across several nodes in a cluster without saving it to a database.

In fact, there is a way. If you can represent that data by using data structures that follow specific criteria, you can replicate it reliably in an eventually consistent fashion. This replication can happen entirely in memory; no database needs to be involved. This gives you a distributed, eventually consistent method of storing and retrieving data.

These eventually consistent data types are called Conflict-Free Replicated Data Types, or CRDTs. CRDTs are an emerging concept. The idea first appeared in a paper in 2011 by Marc Shapiro et al. At this point, CRDTs are not widely used, but interest in them is growing, particularly for use cases in which a system handles very high volumes of data traffic but still needs to be performant.

Akka has its own implementation of CRDTs called *Distributed Data*. This is a new module in Akka, and it is still experiencing some flux. The API is changing as developers iron out the details of how it should work.

The basic idea behind CRDTs in Akka is that you have certain data types. These include Counters, Sets, Maps, and Registers. To be considered CRDTs, these data types must include a conflict-free merge function. This merge function has the job of taking two different states of the data (coming from two different locations in the cluster) and merging them together to create a final result. If this merge can be done without conflict, you can use this data structure to replicate across nodes.

Here's how it works. As each node receives updates to its data, it broadcasts its current state to other nodes. Other nodes receive the updated state, merge it with their own state, and then store the end result.

CRDTs typically work by storing extra information along with the state. Additive operations are often safe, but removal operations become more complex. For example, what happens if you try to remove an element from a Set that has not yet received the update to add that element? How do you resolve that conflict? This is typically handled by making removal an additive operation. Rather than removing an item, you mark that item as removed, but it is still present in the data. This means that your data continually grows. Even as you try to remove information, you are in fact adding information. There are optimizations that you can apply in certain circumstances to help with this.

So how do you use Akka Distributed Data? Let's take a look at how you might replicate some simple session information among nodes in the cluster. In this example, let's assume that you are replicating only the session IDs, which are a custom type that wraps a UUID. We use the ORSet data type for replication. An ORSet, or Observed Remove Set, is a special type of Set that uses a version vector to keep track of the creation of elements. This version vector is then used as part of the merge function to determine causality. In an ORSet, if an add and a remove happen out of order, or concurrently, the version vector will be used to resolve the conflict. You can't remove a record if you haven't yet seen the add for it. If an add and remove happen concurrently, the add wins. Here's how it looks:

```
case class SessionId(value: UUID = UUID.randomUUID())

object SessionManager {
  case class CreateSession(sessionId: SessionId)
  case class SessionCreated(sessionId: SessionId)

  case class TerminateSession(sessionId: SessionId)
  case class SessionTerminated(sessionid: SessionId)

  case object GetSessionIds
  case class SessionIds(ids: Set[SessionId])

  def props() = Props(new SessionManager)
}

class SessionManager extends Actor {
  import SessionManager._

  private val replicator = DistributedData(context.system).replicator
```

```scala
  private val sessionIdsKey = ORSetKey[SessionId]("SessionIds")
  private implicit val cluster = Cluster(context.system)

  override def receive: Receive = {
  case CreateSession(id) =>
    replicator ! Update(
      sessionIdsKey,
      ORSet.empty[SessionId],
      WriteLocal,
      request = Some(sender() -> SessionCreated(id))
    ) {
      existingIds =>
        existingIds + id
    }

  case UpdateSuccess(
    `sessionIdsKey`,
    Some((originalSender: ActorRef, response: SessionCreated))
  ) => originalSender ! response

  case TerminateSession(id) =>
    replicator ! Update(
      sessionIdsKey,
      ORSet.empty[SessionId],
      WriteLocal,
      request = Some(sender() -> SessionTerminated(id))
    ) {
      existingIds =>
        existingIds - id
    }

  case UpdateSuccess(
    `sessionIdsKey`,
    Some((originalSender: ActorRef, response: SessionTerminated))
  ) => originalSender ! response

  case GetSessionIds =>
    replicator ! Get(sessionIdsKey, ReadLocal, request = Some(sender()))

  case result @ GetSuccess(`sessionIdsKey`, Some(originalSender: ActorRef)) =>
    originalSender ! SessionIds(result.get(sessionIdsKey).elements)
  }

}
```

You can see from this code that in order to use data replication, you need to access the replicator. This special actor can be obtained by using the DataReplication extension. You can update replicated data by sending an Update message to the replicator. As soon as the data is updated, you will receive an UpdateSuccess message. You can retrieve replicated data by sending a Get message to the replicator. The replicator will respond with a GetSuccess message.

There are other messages that you can send to the replicator, as well. You can subscribe to updates so that you will be notified when a value changes by using the `Subscribe` message, and you can delete records by using the `Delete` message.

The replicator will take care of replicating your state across the cluster. This actor will be eventually consistent across the cluster. This means on any node in the cluster that runs the `SessionManager`, you can request the list of `SessionIds`, and you will get a list of active sessions. Of course, because this is eventually consistent, the nodes might give you slightly different lists. You can control this eventual consistency by specifying different read/write consistency values.

In the previous example, *local* consistency is specified, which means the replicator only looks at the local node. However, you can specify more strict values that will cause the replicator to ensure that a certain number of nodes must agree on the result before you consider it valid. `ReadAll` and `WriteAll` means that all nodes must agree, but it also affects your availability. If a node is down, the replicator won't be able to reach the required consistency and your request will fail. You can also specify `Read Majority` or `WriteMajority`, which will ensure that the majority of nodes agree on the value. This gives you a nice balance of consistency versus availability.

Graceful Degradation

One of the benefits of breaking your application into microservices is that it enables graceful degradation. Within an application, we enable graceful degradation by setting up failure zones in the application. By creating actors in hierarchies that allow a section of the application to fail without bringing down the entire system, we allow our application to degrade in pieces rather than failing all at once. Microservices enable this same behavior but spread across multiple Java Virtual Machines (JVMs) and potentially multiple machines.

We would like to avoid the situation implied in the old quote "If at first you don't succeed, then perhaps skydiving is not for you." We want our applications to continue even in the face of failure.

In our sample scheduling domain, we can separate out a few services. We have the scheduling engine, the Project Management service, the Person Management service, and the Skills service. This means that if our scheduling engine fails, it doesn't prevent us from adding or removing projects or people. It only prevents us from scheduling people on a project. You can do this within a single monolithic application, by using actors to create failure zones, or you can do it by using microservices.

Graceful degradation means that while portions of an application might fail, the application as a whole can continue to operate, keeping it available even in the face of failure. It also means that noncritical portions of the application can be taken down, perhaps for maintenance or other reasons, without necessarily affecting your users in an adverse way.

Let's take a look at that. The scheduling engine in our system doesn't necessarily need to respond in a rapid fashion. It might be reasonable for a new project to be created but for it to take a period of time, minutes, or maybe even hours, before it returns results. There is no expectation that the moment a project is created it should be scheduled, as well. This means that if that section of the application were in need of some maintenance, perhaps a database upgrade, you could take the entire application down and perform that upgrade. In the meantime, users can still add new people and they can still add new projects; they just won't get the schedule for that project until after the maintenance is completed. And that's OK.

You can use the Circuit Breaker pattern discussed in Chapter 7 to provide graceful degradation. Typically, detection of the failure of an external system is a time-consuming operation. The system might need to wait for a connection to time out. If it did this for every subsequent request until the resource became available again, the system as a whole would take on an additional burden. By using the Circuit Breaker, the system is able to detect the first time a problem occurs and then quickly fail any additional requests until the timeout has elapsed. This helps keep subsequent failing requests from taking longer than they need to, and it also reduces the load on the system so that it can recover. This improves availability because rather than presenting timeout alerts, which can be time consuming, the system instead can quickly inform you about the error and which service is unavailable. Even though a portion of the system is unavailable, it is still responsive, even if all it's doing is notifying you of the error.

Deployment

After you have built your application to support availability using the techniques outlined, you then need to be able to deploy it in a way that maintains that availability. If the deployment process requires that you bring down the entire application suite, you haven't achieved the desired goal.

With a bit of planning and forethought, though, you can come very close to 100 percent service availability, even during deployment.

In Akka, each executable process typically contains a single actor system, which joins the remainder of the processes in the cluster to create a single distributed actor system.

Staged Deployment/Rolling Restarts

One of the most common reasons for nodes to become unavailable in a system isn't an error at all. Rather, it's a normal operational concern: upgrades. When you have a new version of your application or service, you need to deploy it to your production environment at some point.

Automation can be critical here, particularly when you're dealing with microservices. You will not have just a single copy of a monolithic application to deploy, but rather many copies of numerous microservices, potentially even hundreds in a large system. This would be a tedious and error-prone process if it were a manual operation, but with a bit of automation, you can make it simpler and more convenient.

The most commonly used approach with distributed systems is to use *staged deployments*, also called *rolling restarts*. The basic process for a rolling restart looks like this:

1. Select a node in the cluster.
2. Stop routing new traffic to this node.
3. Allow any existing requests to complete. This is sometimes called "draining" the node.
4. Gracefully terminate the application you are planning to upgrade. In an Akka Cluster, this would involve removing the node from the cluster.
5. Copy the new executable to the node.
6. Launch the new executable. In an Akka Cluster, the node would then need to join the cluster.
7. Verify that the node is available and that it is the expected version (a monitoring status page can help here).
8. Begin routing traffic to the new node.
9. Repeat these steps for other nodes.

Rolling restarts require that you have multiple instances of a service running in order to maintain availability. When the node is taken down for deployment, other nodes need to be available to pick up the slack.

If you're using a cluster singleton, you can't maintain availability during an upgrade—the singleton pattern doesn't allow it. However, you can minimize the downtime by allowing other nodes to host the singleton. In this case, when you bring down the current node, the singleton can fail-over to one of the other hosts, exposing only a very short period of downtime.

Blue/Green Deployment

An alternative to the rolling upgrade process is called *blue/green* deployment. For this method, you must have more nodes then you actually need. Usually you would have double the number of nodes that are required for normal operation, with only half of the nodes actually servicing requests at any given time.

In this deployment model, you designate 50 percent of the nodes as "blue," and the other 50 percent as "green." Suppose that your green nodes are currently online and servicing requests. You can then shut down all the blue nodes, upgrade them, bring them back up, and then check them for operational status (remember, no traffic is being routed to them) The final step is to swap the blue set for the green set, making the blue nodes active, and the green nodes inactive. Now you are free to upgrade the green set using the same process.

One big advantage to this process is that if a problem arises with the newly activated set after the switchover, you can simply switch back to the previous set (in this example, the green set) before upgrading them. For this reason it can be beneficial to keep your inactive set on the old version for a period of time while the new version runs, and watch for any issues. Only when you are confident that the new version is stable and working would you upgrade the inactive set.

Crash Recovery/Operational Monitoring

A critical element of availability in a clustered environment is the ability to recognize when a failure has occurred and then respond to it appropriately. Even better is when we can recognize the problem before it occurs and take steps to prevent it. To achieve this, we need to do *operational monitoring*. There are a variety of monitoring tools that you can use, and each of them has its place in a system.

Health Checks and Application Status Pages

Most monitoring tools have one thing in common: they usually rely on some sort of health-check mechanism. Perhaps the most common mechanism for performing health checks is using an HTTP status page.

An application status page is basically a URL that accepts a Get request. When it receives such a request it does any internal checks that are necessary and then returns the result of those checks to indicate whether the application is healthy. This might return HTML, JSON, XML, or whatever is convenient for your environment.

Akka HTTP can help you here by offering a simple and lightweight way of providing those status pages. In fact, it isn't a bad practice to include an Akka HTTP health-check page, even when your application does not otherwise require an HTTP interface. A microservice that communicates entirely by using actors can still benefit from having a few Akka HTTP endpoints for monitoring as well as general maintenance.

So what might a health check look like? What kind of information should be included in such a page?

It is a good idea to include a section that indicates whether external dependencies of the service are available. Can the service communicate with its database? Can it communicate with other external APIs? These checks don't need to be heavy; a simple ping type operation is all you need. And depending on the service, the failure of an external dependency might not represent a failure of the application, which can continue to operate. You will need to judge on a case-by-case basis whether a failed dependency should constitute a failure of the application, or perhaps just a warning or alert.

Another useful piece of information to include on this page is the application version number or commit hash. This can be very helpful for determining whether an upgrade was successful. It can also be useful for tracing errors. If you know the version number, you can eliminate changes to the code that are not part of that version number, which might help you to determine the source of the problem.

Here is a very simple template of what a monitoring page might look like:

```
case class Symptom(description: String)

sealed trait Diagnosis {
  def name: String
}

case class Healthy(name: String) extends Diagnosis

case class Unhealthy(name: String, symptoms: Set[Symptom]) extends Diagnosis

case class HealthReport(versionNumber: String, healthChecks: Seq[Diagnosis])

trait HealthCheck {
  def checkHealth(): Diagnosis
}

class HealthCheckRouting(applicationVersion: String, checks: Seq[HealthCheck])
  extends HealthReportProtocol {
  val routes = {
    path("health") {
      get {
        complete {
          HealthReport(applicationVersion, checks.map(_.checkHealth()))
        }
      }
    }
  }
```

```
    }
  }
```

This routing class will provide a health monitoring page. It builds a `HealthReport` that contains the version information as well as the status of various services in your application that have implemented the `HealthCheck` trait. The details of how these health checks are implemented will be different from service to service, but the basic idea is that when you perform a health check, if there are any problems, they will be returned as `Symptoms` in the `Unhealthy Diagnosis`. Of course if the service is healthy, it will return a `Healthy Diagnosis`. The `HealthReportProtocol` takes the resulting report and converts it to the appropriate format for your use case (e.g., JSON, XML, etc.).

Metrics

Health checks are a great tool for alerting you to issues when they occur, and also for automated tools to monitor in order to take appropriate actions when a problem occurs (like notifying the team). However, they tend to be reactive, in the negative sense, rather than proactive. They inform you that a problem has occurred rather than warning you that a problem will occur. So, how can you detect problems before they occur so that you can take the necessary steps to prevent them?

One way to do this is by using a good metrics system. Usually this comes in the form of a time-series database. It could be a special-purpose database, such as InfluxDB or Graphite, or it can be something more general purpose like Cassandra or SQL, where you have created time-based collections. In either case, the real power comes when you have a good visualization tool that you can use to view your metrics.

A good rule of thumb for any system, Akka based or otherwise, is to wrap timers around entry points to your system. Essentially these timers will record the start and end time of an operation, compute the difference, and then store that in the time-series database. This means that for every operation your system performs, you will know the time it took to perform that operation, and the time at which that operation occurred.

Using this information, you can begin to see patterns within your application. For instance, you can see when your traffic peaks. You can see when operations begin to speed up or slow down. And with that information available, you can notice trends. The best way to see these trends is to put them on a visual graph. Graphs are far easier for visualizing patterns than presenting the information in a table. Looking at those graphs you might notice that when your application reaches a certain number of operations per second, it tends to crash shortly thereafter. Or you might observe that when operations begin to take too long, a system crash is usually not far behind.

This type of information, when combined with other information—CPU usage, memory graphs, application startups, deployments, and more—can reveal things that you might otherwise not have noticed. It is a crucial part of operational monitoring, especially in a large distributed system. You can use it to correlate certain events in your system with failures. You might notice that when your operations begin to drag on for too long, your memory usage spikes. You can then correlate this threshold with application failures. This might lead you to conclude that you need more memory, or it might reveal that the way you are using memory in your application is flawed (a memory leak, for example). Or perhaps you observe that your application was behaving fine until a recent deployment, after which problems began cropping up. From there, you can investigate what changes were introduced in that new version.

The graphs and metrics are just the first step, however. They show you that something is going wrong, but they don't necessarily give you the details about what exactly the problem is. Part of that comes from a human interpreting the data. Humans are very good at recognizing patterns. Although you can have machines monitor for things like thresholds being breached, sometimes the problems that a human detects are not the types of things that machines are good at (at least not yet). Sometimes, a human observer can look at a graph that doesn't cross any monitoring thresholds, and still detect that something looks off. Maybe you aren't using too much memory, but the way that the memory is being used has changed. Perhaps you aren't experiencing too much load, but it is simply more or less than is normal. Although these observations might be meaningless or coincidental, often they can be the first signs of an impending problem. It is therefore important to have a human observer looking at these graphs from time to time, to spot these deviations from the norm.

Logging

After you have detected that something is different in the graphs, the next step is to determine why. This is where logging becomes critical. Your graphs and your health checks are there to alert you to a problem. Your logging is there to help you diagnose it.

Much like with metrics, a good practice is to log as much information as you can any time there is an input to the system. If a REST call is made to the system, log the details of that call. If a top-level actor receives a message, log that message. And of course, if your application throws an exception, be sure to log that exception somewhere.

These logs are going to be where you go when your application is misbehaving. You need to ensure that you have as much information available as possible. If you forget to include the logging, the information won't be there when you need it. It's better to log too much information than not enough, but be aware that too much logging can make it difficult to see what's relevant and what isn't.

Watchdog Tools

When you have your health checks, metrics, and logging in place, the next step is to introduce tools to take that information and automatically act on it so that you don't need to.

First and foremost, you will probably want some sort of notification mechanism. These tools will need to monitor your health checks, and perhaps even your logging and metrics, and alert you through emails, phone calls, chat tools, or other mechanisms when a problem occurs.

Although alerts are important, they can be frustrating, as well. You don't want to be the person getting the call at 3 A.M. on a weekend saying that your system is down and you need to fix it. It would be better if rather than simply alerting you, the tool could also take some corrective action.

If you have built your system using the "let it crash" mentality, when your application does crash, a logical course of action is to restart it. There are tools, available both free and commercially, that will allow this functionality. Tools like Monit, Marathon, ConductR, and more allow you to monitor your application, and in the event of a failure, they can automatically restart it, perhaps even on a different node in the cluster, without the middle-of-the-night phone call. It might not even be necessary to send a notification, or the nature of that notification can change. Rather than call, the system simply sends an email.

This is also an area for which it is important to be watching your graphs and your logs. Depending on how you have configured those restart mechanisms and the nature of the problem, it's possible for your system to limp along for days, restarting constantly, but still managing to service requests. This isn't a good situation. It will work, but you need to do something about it. If you aren't paying attention to the notifications, graphs, and logging, you might never see that a problem has occurred. No one is going to phone you to complain, because from an outsider's perspective, the system is working.

Operational monitoring is not about a single tool that does all the work for you. There are many different types of monitoring, and each of them provides a different feature set and a different kind of information. The combination of these tools is what allows you to really get a sense of the ebb and flow of your system. Health checks and metrics alert you to a problem, logs can help you diagnose the problem, and watchdog tools can automatically respond to the problem. On their own, each tool is useful, but together they are invaluable.

Conclusion

We have now shown how actor-based systems have different requirements: just logging is not enough, and static testing before deployment is insufficient as well.

With proper monitoring, however, availability can be ensured, and the overall health of your system made immediately visible despite rapidly changing load (even in the face of the system itself being continually upgraded).

Having all of these benefits while still retaining high performance, however, requires careful attention. This will be the topic of Chapter 9, as we add the final piece you need for building your own actor-based systems.

CHAPTER 9
Performance

Performance tuning an Akka application begins as it would with any application: first you isolate the areas of the application that have the highest cost in terms of time, and then you strive to reduce that cost.

Given that we always have a limited amount of time to apply to tuning, it makes good sense to begin with the greatest cost. Of course, it is difficult to know what this is without measurement. Therefore, as you would with any application, your first step in tuning Akka is generally to measure what takes a long time.

Many excellent performance and latency measurement tools exist for the Java Virtual Machine (JVM), and you can apply any of them to an Akka application. For instance, you can use the Gatling tool to measure the performance of an Akka application with an HTTP interface in the same way as any non-Akka application, and you can apply ScalaMeter to specific code segments.

In addition to the usual statistics on number of requests served, latency, and so on, there are a few special statistics unique to Akka that might be helpful.

Given that a slow consumer in an Akka application can become a serious runtime issue, you might need to measure mailbox size to ensure that any actor (or group of actors) isn't growing its mailbox beyond reasonable bounds.

The time that it takes each message to be processed by a given actor is also very useful —when used in conjunction with information about the frequency of a message, it can help you narrow down bottlenecks. For instance, if a certain message (say, `Compu teInvoice`) takes a relatively long time (as measured by, for instance, a `ScalaMeter` microbenchmark), but is not that common or timing-critical, it's not a good candidate to tune. A much more common message, say `LookupInvoice`, which takes a relatively short amount of time but is under heavy volume, might be a better choice.

As you can see, you'll need to be able to simulate a typical load on your application, and perhaps even predict what an extreme load would look like so that you can measure under realistic conditions.

Isolating Bottlenecks

There's an old story about a factory that was having a problem with one of its huge machines. The factory manager called in an expert, who walked straight over to one part of the machine, took out a crescent wrench, and tightened one bolt a quarter-turn. The machine resumed running properly immediately, and the expert left. A few days later, the factory received an invoice from the expert for $5,000. The factory manager called the expert and complained, "Five thousand dollars? You were here for only five minutes!" The expert calmly replied, "I'll send you a new invoice with a breakdown." A short while later, another invoice arrived that said "1) Tighten bolt, $5; 2) Knowing which bolt to tighten, $4,995."

Akka tuning is a bit like this: often you need to make only a tiny change to get the results you need, but knowing *which* change to make is the trick.

The first step in tuning most scalability or performance issues is to identify the bottleneck. What are you running out of that causes the system to not perform the way you want it to? Is it memory? It is threads or cores? Is it I/O capacity?

To identify the bottleneck, you often need a combination of logging, monitoring, and live inspection, and tools such as VisualVM or YourKit can be essential for this.

If you eliminate all the usual suspects in JVM tuning (running out of memory, leaking objects, running out of file handles) and know that the Akka portion of your project contains the bottleneck, then and only then can you consider tuning Akka itself.

Keep in mind that JVM tuning issues can be much more subtle: for example, the garbage collector taking too much processing time and "thrashing" by running too often is not as obvious as an actual failure. JVM tuning is beyond the scope of this book, but many good resources exist.

Tuning Akka

After you've identified a potential area for tuning, what options do you have available? There are three major areas that you can tackle. Let's take a look at each one.

Reduce or Isolate Blocking Sections

Even in a highly concurrent actor-based application, many blocking operations can still exist—an actor might need to access a nonasynchronous JDBC data source, for instance. Although the most common blocking operations are IO-based, there are others that hold the current thread captive, thereby reducing the threads available for other processes to continue, and slowing the entire system. We will elaborate on this further when we discuss dispatchers.

Make the Message Process in Less Time

Because actors are all about processing messages, anything you can do to reduce the processing time of each message is a benefit to the entire system. If it is possible to break the problem into smaller problems that can be tackled concurrently, this is often a winning strategy, and it has the added benefit of separating logic into smaller and more isolated sections. Actors are inexpensive to create, and messages between actors (especially on the same JVM) are also inexpensive, so breaking up a problem from one actor to a group of them is a good tactic, generally. Often this leads to opportunities for increased parallelism, as will be discussed shortly.

Engage More Actors on Processing the Messages

Another strategy, if the problem allows it, is to increase the number of instances of the same actor working on the messages to be handled; for example, to use a pool router to distribute work among a group of identical actors. This works only if the problem is compute-bound—that is, not constrained by external I/O, and if each instance of the message is entirely independent (it does not depend on state contained in the actor to be processed). The limit of this technique is essentially the number of available cores; increasing the number of actors much beyond this won't help. However, it is possible to distribute the pool of actors across a cluster, effectively getting more cores than a single machine can bring to bear. This is a common Akka pattern, and if you apply it properly, this capability forms the basis of much of Akka's power in distributed systems.

This is very different from the technique of simply load-balancing requests among a group of identical nodes. Distributed actors can apply more than one node's power to servicing a single request, which is beyond the reach of a simple node-balancing solutiuon.

Dispatchers

Dispatchers are a critical component for tuning Akka. You can think of dispatchers as the engine that powers actor systems. Without them, the system doesn't run. And if you are not careful with them, the system doesn't perform.

The job of the dispatcher is to manage threads, allocate those threads to actors, and give those actors opportunities to process their mailboxes. How this works depends on the type of dispatcher as well as what configuration settings you have used for the dispatcher. So what kinds of dispatchers are available?

The Standard Dispatcher

The standard dispatcher is the one most commonly used. It is a good, general-purpose dispatcher. This dispatcher utilizes a customizable pool of threads. These threads will be shared among the actors managed by the dispatcher. Depending on the number of actors and the number of threads, the actors might have restricted access to the threads because they might be currently in use by other actors.

A simple configuration for this dispatcher looks like the following:

```
custom-dispatcher {
  type = Dispatcher
  executor = "fork-join-executor"
  fork-join-executor {
    parallelism-min = 4
    parallelism-factor = 3.0
    parallelism-max = 64
  }
  throughput = 5
}
```

In the preceding example, `throughput` is set to 5, meaning at most 5 messages will be processed before the thread of execution will be available for other actors; this factor varies considerably based on your specific requirements.

The example also uses a `fork-join-executor`; however, that is not the only option. You can also use a `thread-pool-executor`. Depending on which you use, the tuning parameters are slightly different. You can use `thread-pool-executor` like this:

```
custom-dispatcher {
  type = Dispatcher
  executor = "thread-pool-executor"
  thread-pool-executor {
    core-pool-size-min = 4
    core-pool-size-max = 64
  }
  throughput = 5
}
```

Each executor has a minimum and maximum thread value to ensure that the number of available threads remains within this boundary. Each also has a factor. The factor is a multiplier. To calculate the number of available threads, you multiply the number of cores on the machine by the factor and then bind it between the minimum and maximum. This means that if you move your application to a machine with more cores, you will have more threads, assuming the minimum/maximum allows it. Note that with a `fork-join-executor`, the `parallelism-max` is not the maximum number of threads; rather, it is the maximum number of hot or active threads. This is an important distinction because the `fork-join-executor` can create additional threads as they become blocked, leading to an explosion of threads.

Your decision as to whether to use a `fork-join-executor` or a `thread-pool-executor` is largely based on whether the operations in that dispatcher will be blocking. A `fork-join-executor` gives you a maximum number of *active* threads, whereas a `thread-pool-executor` gives you a fixed number of threads. If threads are blocked, a `fork-join-executor` will create more, whereas a `thread-pool-executor` will not. For blocking operations, you are generally better off with a `thread-pool-executor` because it prevents your thread counts from exploding. More "reactive" operations are better in a `fork-join-executor`.

Throughput is an interesting option. The throughput value determines how many messages an actor is allowed to process before the dispatcher will attempt to release the thread to another actor. It determines how fair the actors will be in their sharing of the threads. A low throughput number like 1 indicates that the actors are as fair as possible. With a value of 1, each actor will process one message and then yield the thread to another actor. On the other hand, a value of 100 is much less fair. Each actor will occupy the thread for 100 messages before yielding. When should you use a high number and when should you use a low number? You'll need to play with the numbers in your system to really find the sweet spot, but there are a few things to consider.

Each time you yield the thread, a context switch must happen. These context switches can be expensive if they happen often enough. This means that depending on your application and the size of your messages, too many context switches can begin to have a significant impact on the performance of your application. If your dispatcher has a large number of very fast messages flowing through it all the time, those context switches can hurt. In this case, you might want to tune the throughput number to be higher. Because the messages are fast, you won't be stuck with idle actors waiting for long periods of time. Their wait times will be fairly low, despite the high throughput value. And by increasing that throughput, you will have allowed the system to minimize the impact of context switching, which can help improve the system's performance.

However, if your messages are not fast and take a long time to process, a high throughput value can be crippling. In this case, you can end up with many of your actors sitting idle for long periods of time while they wait for the slow messages to push through. Context switching isn't hurting you much because your messages are long running. This is where you want to tune your dispatcher for fairness. A low throughput value is probably what you want here. This will allow the long-running actors to process a single message and then yield to one of the waiting actors.

Using this dispatcher in your code is as simple as calling the `withDispatcher` method on the `Props` for your actor, as demonstrated here:

```
val actor = system.actorOf(Props(new MyActor).withDispatcher("custom-dispatcher"))
```

Pinned Dispatcher

In certain use cases, sharing threads can be detrimental to your actor system. In this case, you might opt to use a pinned dispatcher. Rather than using a thread pool for the actors, a pinned dispatcher allocates a single thread per actor. This eliminates the worry over tuning your throughput and thread counts, but it does come at a cost.

Threads aren't free. There is a finite amount of hardware on which to run those threads, and they need to share that hardware. This sharing comes with its own form of context switching. A large number of threads means more context switching as those threads contend for the same resources. There are also limits to the number of threads you can create. Even though the concept of one thread per actor sounds appealing, in reality its uses are much more limited than you might expect. You are usually better off going with the standard dispatcher rather than a pinned dispatcher.

Another consideration with a pinned dispatcher is the fact that it allocates only a single thread per actor. If your actor is not mixing concurrency techniques, this is not a problem, but often actors might make use of futures internally. When doing this, it is common to use the actor's dispatcher as an execution context, but remember that in this case the actor is being assigned just a single thread on which to operate. This means that using the actor's dispatcher is going to give you access to only that single thread. Depending on the circumstances, this can either result in a performance hit because your futures now must operate in a single-threaded manner, or in some cases it might even result in a deadlock as multiple concurrent pieces of the system contend for the same thread.

So where are the right places to use a pinned dispatcher? Pinned dispatchers are useful for situations in which you have one actor, or a small number of actors, that need to be able to go "as fast as possible." For example, if your system has a set of operations that are considered "high priority," you probably don't want those operations sharing resources. You probably want to avoid a thread pool because your high-priority operations would then be coupled to each other (and possibly other actors) by sharing a thread. They can create contention for the threads, which could cause them to slow down. In that case, a pinned dispatcher for those operations might be a good solution. A pinned dispatcher means that the actors don't need to wait for one another.

Balancing Dispatcher

A balancing dispatcher is one that will redistribute work from busy actors to idle actors. It does this by using a shared mailbox. All messages go into a single mailbox. The dispatcher can then move messages from one actor to the other, allowing them to share the load.

However, a balancing dispatcher has limited use cases, and is often not the right choice. Due to the work sharing nature of the dispatcher, you can't use it as a general-purpose mailbox. All actors that use the dispatcher must be able to process all messages in the mailbox. This typically limits its use to actors of the same type.

Otherwise, a balancing dispatcher works much the same as the standard dispatcher. It uses a thread pool that you can tune in the same way as the standard dispatcher.

Balancing dispatchers can be useful for cases in which you have multiple actors of the same type and you want to share the workload between them, but other approaches are usually superior.

Calling-Thread Dispatcher

The calling-thread dispatcher is designed for testing. In this case, no thread pool is allocated. All operations are performed on the same thread that sent the original message. This is useful in tests for removing a lot of the concurrency concerns that make testing difficult. When everything operates on the same thread, concurrency is no longer an issue.

Of course, removing the concurrency of the system is an artificial situation. In your live system, you will not be operating in a single-threaded manner, so even though simulating this might be useful for tests, it can give you a false impression of how the system behaves. Worse, it can also lead to deadlocks in your actors as they suddenly find themselves needing to asynchronously wait but are unable to do so. It is generally better, even in tests, to use a proper thread pool–based dispatcher.

In addition, the Akka TestKit provides many facilities for testing that make explicit use of a calling-thread dispatcher largely unnecessary.

When to Use Your Own Dispatchers

When you create an actor without explicitly assigning a dispatcher, that actor is created as part of the default dispatcher. As such, it will share a thread pool with all other actors. For many actors, this is perfectly acceptable. There are certain conditions, however, that warrant a separate dispatcher.

You want to try to avoid blocking or long-running operations as much as possible inside of actors. These blocking operations can have a significant effect on the availability of threads in your thread pool, and they can hinder the performance of the application. But this isn't always possible. There are times when despite your best efforts, you must block. In these cases, you should use a separate dispatcher.

Let's begin by analyzing what happens when you don't use a separate dispatcher. It is fairly common when building a system to provide a special "monitoring" or "health check" operation. These operations might do something fairly simple just to verify the application is running and responsive. It can be as simple as a ping/pong test. Or it can be more complex, including checking database connections and testing various requests. For the moment, we will consider the simple ping/pong test. This operation should be very fast. It doesn't need to communicate with a database, or do any computation:

```
object Monitoring {
  case object Ping
  case object Pong
}

class Monitoring extends Actor {
  import Monitoring._

  override def receive: Receive = {
    case Ping =>
      sender() ! Pong
  }
}
```

What if, within the same API, we have another, more complex operation? This operation needs to read data from a database, transform it, and eventually return it. And let's further assume that the database driver we are using is a blocking driver:

```
class DataReader extends Actor {
  import DataReader._

  override def receive: Actor.Receive = {
    case ReadData =>
      sender() ! Data(readFromDatabase())
  }

  private def readFromDatabase() = {
    // This reads from a database in a blocking fashion.
    // It then transforms the result into the required format.
    ...
  }
}
```

If these two operations are performed in the same dispatcher, how do they affect each other? If several requests to the long-running operation come in at the same time, it is possible that those requests will block all the available threads in the dispatcher. These threads will be unavailable until the operation completes. This means that when the monitoring service makes the ping/pong request to verify that the API is up and available, it will be delayed or it will fail. There are no available threads on which to perform the ping/pong request, so the service must wait.

In this very simple example, there is coupling between the two operations. Even though these operations perform very different tasks and in many respects are entirely unrelated, they are coupled to the resources that they share—in this case, the thread pool. As a result of this coupling, poor performance on one of the operations can cause poor performance on the other. This is probably not desirable.

To solve this problem, you can introduce a separate dispatcher. By putting the actors that perform each task on a separate dispatcher, you break this coupling. Now, each operation has its own pool of threads. So, when the long-running operation blocks all of its available threads, there are still additional threads, in a separate dispatcher, available to perform the ping/pong request. Thus, monitoring can remain operational even when other parts of the system have become blocked, as illustrated here:

```
data-reader-dispatcher {
  type = Dispatcher
  executor = "thread-pool-executor"
  thread-pool-executor {
    core-pool-size-min = 4
    core-pool-size-max = 16
  }
  throughput = 1
}


// For monitoring, because it is a very fast operation,
// it is sufficient to leave it in the default dispatcher.
val monitoring = system.actorOf(Monitoring.props())

// For our data reader, we have a separate dispatcher created to manage
// operations for reading data.
val reader = system.actorOf(
  DataReader.props().withDispatcher("data-reader-dispatcher"))
```

There are many cases for which you might want to look at using a separate dispatcher. A separate dispatcher makes it possible for you to tune groups of actors independently. If one group of actors requires a high-throughput setting, whereas a different group would work better with a low throughput setting, separating them into different dispatchers will enable this independent tuning. Or, if you have one set of actors that receives a large volume of messages and another that receives a lower volume, you might want to split them simply to be more fair. And what about priority? If certain messages are high priority, you might want to isolate them in their own dispatcher so that they are not contending with other actors for threads.

The key is that you don't want to use the same dispatcher everywhere. One of the primary mistakes people make when starting out with Akka is using the default dispatcher for all actors. This can result in a system that is very unresponsive, despite the fact that it isn't consuming a lot of hardware resources. You can end up with a system in which your CPU is essentially idle, and yet the system is not responding. Creating separate dispatchers and tuning them for specific use cases is the first step toward solving this problem.

Increase Parallelism

Increasing parallelism is another approach to tuning Akka. Often, an increase in parallelism is required before increasing the number of actors processing a request can really be of help, but parallelism, of course, does not necessarily mean actors.

How to increase parallelism in any given algorithm is a wide topic and could warrant an entire book of its own, but some general principles apply. Reducing contention by reducing coupling and shared data is one key element; breaking the problem into those portions of the problem that do not depend on others having completed is another.

Assuming that you are able to refactor an algorithm to permit more parallelism, you will still be, as discussed a bit earlier, constrained by the number of cores available on any single node as to how much true parallelism you can achieve—this is where the Actor Model allows you to surpass limitations that had existed before.

A single request or algorithm can now have its parallelizable elements distributed— that is, handled by more than one node. Each node can then bring to bear all of the cores available on that node, allowing the total parallelism of a problem to be taken much higher than is possible on a single node.

The easiest application of this is often an algorithm that is compute-bound; in other words, it cannot be processed any faster on a single node because it runs out of CPU resources. By breaking that algorithm into portions that don't depend on one another and distributing those portions, you can effectively run the problem on a larger "machine" than any one node can provide.

Not every problem is compute-bound, however; many are I/O bound on data access from some kind of persistent store. In this case, the distributed domain-driven design (DDDD) pattern can be applied, allowing the data to be wrapped with instances of actors, and held in memory. Just like the compute-bound problem gets more CPU applied to it than any one machine could bring to bear, the distributed-domain problem gets more *memory* available to it than is available on any one machine, and converts an I/O-bound problem into something more closely resembling a compute-bound problem.

There is often an element of persistence needed in any case, though—perhaps an event journal must be emitted and consumed by the actors in our system. If the actor needing such access is on a different node, you again end up I/O bound, sometimes on the network instead of the disk.

Conclusion

In this chapter, you have seen how careful tuning and consideration of performance avoids critical bottlenecks that can otherwise counteract the advantages of a highly scalable and available actor-based system.

You have now seen all of the essential aspects of building power applications with Akka and the Actor Model, from the most granular to the highest levels.

Afterword

We started this book with the assertion that the ideas of concurrency and distribution are fundamental to modern software development. The classical model of computation builds an illusion for us that is not much like the real world, or particularly valuable in a distributed and concurrent environment.

As we have seen, though, the Actor Model builds on a different paradigm, one that fits the reality of the world much better and is especially well suited to reasoning about and building systems whose components are location- and behavior-independent of each other.

Actors are a very powerful abstraction, but they are quite unlike normal imperative or even functional approaches to application development. Applied correctly, they provide a means to easily scale your application, both in terms of its ability to handle load and its ability to handle complex, multistage computations. Applied incorrectly, they can make your application complex and hard to reason about—and therefore hard to maintain.

The difference is in the design patterns.

There are many similarities between good actor patterns and good reactive microservice architectures. Reactive microservice architectures are applied "in the large" as a high-level abstraction to build systems; actor patterns are applied "in the small," within (and between) individual services.

However, if done well, both share the attributes of isolation, independent action and autonomy, resilience, preservation of private state, and asynchronous message-based communication with the rest of the system. As a result, reactive microservice systems compose quite naturally from services composed of actors.

Just as with microservices, the art is in selecting the appropriate means for each element to communicate with the others, finding the right blend of integration while maintaining isolation.

Like reactive microservice systems, though, the added costs of actor-based systems can outstrip the derived benefits if specific guidelines are not followed. Throughout the book, we have tried to point out where certain patterns can result in more disadvantages than advantages, hopefully saving you from having to experience these costs for yourself.

This book has attempted to describe the most important actor patterns, specifically in regards to their use in the Akka library. We believe that if you follow and extend these patterns, you will create applications (and systems) that are scalable, resilient, flexible, and yet easy to maintain over the long term.

References

"Alan Kays Definition Of Object Oriented." Last modified April 18, 2014. *http://c2.com/cgi/wiki?AlanKaysDefinitionOfObjectOriented.*

"Alan Kay On Messaging." Last modified November 12, 2014. *http://c2.com/cgi/wiki?AlanKayOnMessaging.*

Allen, Jamie. *Effective Akka*. Sebastopol: O'Reilly Media, 2013.

Avram, Abel, and Floyd Marinescu. *Domain-Driven Design Quickly*. Lulu.com, 2007.

Evans, Eric. *Domain-Driven Design: Tackling Complexity in the Heart of Software.* Boston: Addison-Wesley, 2003.

Hewitt, Carl, Peter Bishop, and Richard Steiger. "A universal modular ACTOR formalism for artificial intelligence." *Proceedings of the 3rd International Joint Conference on Artificial Intelligence* (1973): 235-245.

Hewitt, Carl, Erik Meijer, and Clemens Szyperski. "Hewitt, Meijer and Szyperski: The Actor Model (everything you wanted to know…)." *https://www.youtube.com/watch?v=7erJ1DV_Tlo.*

Malawski, Konrad. "Lambda Days 2015 - Konrad Malawski - Need for Async(..)." *https://www.youtube.com/watch?v=Q_0z2v3QJg4.*

Index

domain-driven design (see DDD)
fault tolerance (see fault tolerance)
languages supported by, 17
performance (see performance)
remoting (see remoting)
scalability (see scalability)
support for, 19
testing (see TestKit)
Akka Circuit Breaker, 128-131, 150
Akka Cluster, 128
Akka cluster sharding, 128
Akka HTTP, 27, 29
Akka Persistence, 95, 100, 114, 137
Akka Streams, 29, 80-90
    back pressure, 87
    example using, 88-90
    flow, 85
    junctions, 86
    RunnableGraph, 84-85
    sink, 82-84
    source for, 81-82
Akka Typed, 31
Apache Kafka queuing system, 78
application status pages, 152-154
ask method, 30
Ask pattern, 57-62
asynchronous nature of reality, 1-3
At Least Once delivery, 94-97, 137, 139
At Most Once delivery, 94
autodowning, 25
availability, 141-156
    cluster-aware routers for, 144-146
    distributed data for, 146-149
    during deployment, 150-152
    for microservices, 142
    for monolithic applications, 142
    operational monitoring for, 152-156

B

back pressure, 78, 87
balancing dispatchers, 165
bang (see tell method)
become operation, 20, 31, 50-52
behavior of actors
    changing, 8-10, 20, 31
    type for (see Akka Typed)
Bishop, Peter ("Universal Modular Actor Formalism for Artificial Intelligence"), 3
blocking bounded mailboxes, 74

blocking operations
    isolating, 107
    reducing, 160
blue/green deployment, 152
books and publications
    about Actor Model, 3
    about domain-driven design, 33
bottlenecks, isolating, 160
    (see also performance)
bounded contexts, 42-44, 126-128, 142
bounded mailboxes, 74-75
bulkheading, 123-126

C

calling-thread dispatchers, 165
CAP theorem, 112
child actors, 7-8, 20-21, 31
circuit breakers (see Akka Circuit Breaker)
cluster sharding, 26-27, 107-117
    actors in, 109-110
    aggregate roots, 113-114
    consistency with, 111-112, 115-117
    distribution of shards, 111
    passivation with, 114
    persistence with, 114
    scalability boundary in, 112
    shard key, 107, 110
cluster singleton, 99-102, 151
cluster-aware routers, 144-146
clustering, 23-27
    (see also remoting)
    convergence in, 24
    distributed domain with, 26
    examples of, 24
    leader for, 25
    management of, 24
    rebalancing of, 25
    seed nodes for, 23
    singleton for, 27
    split-brain situation in, 25
    unreachable nodes in, 24
commands, 62-63
concurrency
    Actor Model for, 14
    with actors, 52
    compared to parallelism, 92
    with futures, 52-57
    potential problems with, 45, 48, 52
    with routers, 70-73

(see also clustering)
replicator, 148
replyTo actor, 60
repositories, 39-41
resources (see books and publications; website
    resources)
Restart directive, 133
restarting applications, 136, 156
RESTful web services, 29
Resume directive, 133
rolling restarts, 151
routers, 70-73, 144-146
RunnableGraph, for Akka Streams, 84-85

S

Scala, Akka written in, 17
scalability, 102-107
    Actor Model for, 104, 106
    blocking operations, isolating, 107
    cluster sharding with, 107, 112
    compared to elasticity, 105
    consistency affecting, 107
    global consistency incompatible with, 93
    global state, avoiding, 106
    horizontal and vertical, 103
    monitoring with, 105, 107
    relationship to performance, 102-103
    sequential operations, avoiding, 106
    shared state, avoiding, 106
scalability boundary, 112
seed nodes, 23
sequential operations, avoiding, 106
serialization, 22
service-level agreement (SLA), failure to meet,
    122, 128
    (see also fault tolerance)
services
    bounded contexts as, 43-44
    domain (see domain services)
shard key, 107, 110
sharding of clusters (see cluster sharding)
shared kernel, 142
shared state, 106
singleton, cluster, 27
sink, for Akka Streams, 82-84
SLA (service-level agreement), failure to meet,
    122, 128
    (see also fault tolerance)
slow consumer problem

back pressure for, 78
    mailbox settings for, 73-80
    work pulling for, 75-78
source, for Akka Streams, 81-82
split-brain situation, in clustering, 25
staged deployment, 151
state
    changing, 8-10, 20
    encapsulating, 46-57
    maintaining, Actor Model for, 14
    persisting, 114
state objects, 49-50
status pages, 152-154
Steiger, Richard ("Universal Modular Actor
    Formalism for Artificial Intelligence"), 3
Stop directive, 133
storage (see repositories)
streams, 68-70
    Akka Streams (see Akka Streams)
    multiple, processing with routers, 70-73
supervisor actors (see parent actors)
supervisor strategy (supervisorStrategy),
    132-136

T

tell method, 30
"Tell, Don't Ask" principle, 40
TestKit, 27-28
threads (see dispatchers)
throughput, 67-68
timeouts, potential problems with, 59
traits, 29, 32
    concurrency handled with, 48
    repositories as, in Scala, 40
transactions, 92
tuning, 160-161
    (see also performance)
Typed project, Akka (see Akka Typed)

U

ubiquitous language, 34
unbecome operation, 31
unbounded mailboxes, 73
"Universal Modular Actor Formalism for Arti-
    ficial Intelligence" (Hewitt; Bishop; Steiger),
    3

V

Value Objects, 37
Vaughn, Vernon ("Implementing Domain-Driven Design"), 33
vector clocks, 24

W

watchdog tools, 156

website resources
    for this book, xi
    Reactive Manifesto, 18
work pulling, 75-78
worker actors, 75-78
wrapper actor, 53, 57

About the Authors

Michael Nash is director of capabilities at Lightbend. For more than 30 years, he has designed, developed, shipped, and consulted on software development projects for clients of all shapes and sizes. As an advocate for software craftsmanship with expertise in project management and architecture, he was among the earliest adopters of the Typesafe Stack, with more than five years' experience working with Scala, Akka, and Spray. He dedicates the majority of his spare time to working in the Typesafe Reactive Platform, speaking at conferences, and writing books on the software business.

Wade Waldron is a senior consultant at Lightbend, where he works with clients to provide knowledge and expertise on the Lightbend Reactive Platform. Outside of Lightbend, Wade has spent the past nine years building rock-solid software and games, with a strong focus on test-driven design, domain-driven design, service-oriented architecture, event-driven architecture, and agile development.

Colophon

The animal on the cover of *Applied Akka Patterns* is a common teal or Eurasian teal (*Anas crecca*), a duck common throughout Europe and Asia. The color teal is named after this bird—during breeding season, males of the species have vivid blue-green plumage around their eyes. The teal is part of a group known as "dabbling ducks," which feed primarily at the surface or by upending themselves in shallow water.

The Eurasian teal is sexually dimorphic: females are primarily brown with dark bars and white-tipped tail feathers, while males have a gray body with thin, dark striations, brown and white wings, a chestnut-colored head, and the aforementioned teal eyespot. Outside of breeding season, males moult their feathers to make their coloring much less vivid (known as "eclipse plumage"). These birds are among the smallest ducks, averaging 8 to 12 inches long and around 12 ounces in weight.

Teals live in a freshwater habitat of ponds, small lakes, and wetlands. They nest on the ground in deep hollows concealed by dense vegetation. During breeding season (roughly March to May), they eat a diet of small crustaceans, insects, larvae, worms, and fish fry. At other times of year, however, teals consume aquatic vegetation and other plants. They migrate each winter to the Mediterranean, southern Asia, and Africa, and return to temperate regions in northern Europe and Asia to mate.

Many of the animals on O'Reilly covers are endangered; all of them are important to the world. To learn more about how you can help, go to *animals.oreilly.com*.

The cover image is from Wood's *Illustrated Natural History*. The cover fonts are URW Typewriter and Guardian Sans. The text font is Adobe Minion Pro; the heading font is Adobe Myriad Condensed; and the code font is Dalton Maag's Ubuntu Mono.

Learn from experts.
Find the answers you need.

Sign up for a **10-day free trial** to get **unlimited access** to all of the content on Safari, including Learning Paths, interactive tutorials, and curated playlists that draw from thousands of ebooks and training videos on a wide range of topics, including data, design, DevOps, management, business—and much more.

Start your free trial at:
oreilly.com/safari

CPSIA information can be obtained
at www.ICGtesting.com
Printed in the USA
BVOW09s1334201216

471372BV00021B/382/P